DAVID O. HARRISON

C.S. LEWIS

MERE CHRISTIANITY

IN EVERYDAY ENGLISH

AN EASY-TO-READ VERSION OF A LITERARY CLASSIC

PUBLISHED BY THRIVE! BOOKS

Title: Mere Christianity.

Author: Lewis, C. S. [Clive Staples] (1898-1963)

Date of first publication: 1952

TABLE OF CONTENTS

A SPECIAL OFFER

Thank you for purchasing this book (or perhaps you received it as a gift)! It is my earnest prayer that you will be encouraged by what you read.

If you are willing, once you have finished reading this book, please leave a review on Amazon. Simply go to: **amzn.to/3L1wrv7** or scan the QR code below.

As a thank you, if you email a screenshot of your review to **dohauthor@gmail.com**, along with your mailing address, we will send you a free copy of another title, *WHAT'S NEXT? HEAVEN, HELL, NOTHING?*

This Speccial Offer expires September 30, 2024.

Additionally, if you have any constructive comments you would like to offer (content, grammar, references, etc.), I would be thrilled if you would contact me.

David Harison

THRIVE! BOOKS

ABOUT THE AUTHOR

What people are saying…

THE PILGRIM'S PROGRESS IN EVERYDAY ENGLISH

 Faith Builder

☆☆☆☆☆ **Very readable.**

Reviewed in the United States on December 26, 2023

A lot has changed in the last 350 years, but not Bunyan's message. An excellent read.

MERE CHRISTIANITY IN EVERYDAY ENGLISH

 Mr. Jerry W. Gammon

☆☆☆☆☆ **Make Lewis Come Alive**

Reviewed in the United States on December 28, 2023

Verified Purchase

If you love C.S. Lewis but have a difficult time understanding some of his archaic language, you need this modern English version by David Harrison. Mr. Harrison takes the language of mid-twentieth century England and gives it an update making Lewis more understandable and enjoyable to the modern reader. A great read.

 thomas klema

☆☆☆☆☆ **Profound**

Reviewed in the United States on February 19, 2024

Verified Purchase

Plumb the depths of the reasons for the Christian faith. I have given this book as a gift to many people searching for truth. It never disappoints.

 Monty

☆☆☆☆☆ **Finally!**

Reviewed in the United States on March 1, 2024

Verified Purchase

I am so impressed Mr. Harrison has done what I wish had been done before. He took a marvelous work that, for some folks, like myself, can be lost in the language used in some parts of the book. Lewis' Mere Christianity & The Screwtape Letters have a profound message that people like myself can get a better understanding by rewording parts in a more modern vernacular that can be absorbed deeper both mentally and spiritually.
Thank you Mr. David Harrison. Well done sir !

THE SCREWTAPE LETTERS IN EVERYDAY ENGLISH

 Penelope Zelasko

⭐⭐⭐⭐⭐ **Great alternative to the original**

Reviewed in the United States on March 7, 2024

Verified Purchase

I didn't realize this existed until I started searching. I purchased a Screwtape letters by CS Lewis, but found the British language difficult to read. David Harrison is a genius and making things come to life when your culture is very and you can't understand the original.

 Kindle Customer

⭐⭐⭐⭐⭐ **C S Lewis is always amazing**

Reviewed in the United States on January 11, 2024

Verified Purchase

I ordered two so my husband and I could read together. The language is easier to read than C S Lewis's first editions. Quick delivery.

DAVID HARRISON was born and raised in England and emigrated to Canada in 1973 at the age of 21.

When he was 35, David became a Christ-follower. He is married and the father of two adult children. He attended a Brethren Bible Chapel in Scarborough for 25 years, ten of those years as an elder.

For 23 years David ran a successful audiovisual integration company in Toronto, Canada, catering primarily to universities, banks, and law firms.

In 2006 David founded Bus Stop Bible Studies[1], a ministry which used public transit advertising panels to display messages of encouragement from the Word of God to many millions of people in Canada.

---

[1] bit.ly/BSBSIMAGINE

For 10 years David was the Board Chair of Daystar Native Christian Outreach, based on Manitoulin Island.

Now 'retired', David and his wife, Wendy, run a bed & Breakfast in Muskoka, and David (who failed miserably in English at school) has taken to writing as a hobby.

Contact: dohauthor@gmail.com

DEDICATION

This book is dedicated to those whom God has chosen to make my life complete, my wife Wendy, our children, Krista and Daniel, our son-in-law Dan, and our grandchildren Jack and Levi.

Praise God from whom all blessing flow!

WHY THIS BOOK?

C.S. Lewis, the renowned Professor of English at Oxford University, was a literary giant.

Clive Staples Lewis authored many famous novels including the Chronicles of Narnia series and The Screwtape Letters. The most recent estimate for sales of his books is in excess of 200 million copies.

Lewis was born in 1898 in Belfast, Ireland, while I came into the world fifty-three years later in Worcester Park, England. Lewis endured the horrors of trench warfare at the Somme during World War I. I was conceived six years after the end of World War II. Lewis found solace in Christ at the age of 33, deeply influenced by his dear friend J.R.R. Tolkien and other spiritual companions. Similarly, it wasn't until I reached the age of 35, also influenced by friends, that God broke through my hard, prideful shell and radically changed my life.

In 1973, I embarked on a new chapter by emigrating to Canada. It was there that I encountered the captivating Canadian accent, which I grew fond of during my time working with friends in London. Upon arriving in Canada, I diligently shed my English accent and embraced this "new language" as my own. Sometimes, when we throw a party, I delight in presenting a list of thirty everyday words from my native tongue and watching people try to guess their meanings.

Now here I am, someone who flunked high school English, daring to revise C.S. Lewis' most significant work, which has practically become a sacred text. Why, might you wonder? Let me explain.

When I first read MERE CHRISTIANITY, I couldn't help but ponder if the average North American reader could fully grasp the essence of this book without an English-to-"English" dictionary at their side. I even found myself Googling the meaning of some of Lewis's colloquialisms from the 1940s. Even Lewis acknowledged the shifting nature of language and word usage over time, and I've taken the liberty to present you with an original paragraph of his work, alongside my own "simple English" interpretation. I have also added several footnotes for further clarity.

ORIGINAL TEXT:

The word gentleman originally meant something recognisable; one who had a coat of arms and some landed property. When you called someone "a gentleman" you were not paying him a compliment, but merely stating a fact. If you said he was not "a gentleman" you were not insulting him but giving information.

A gentleman, once it has been spiritualized and refined out of its old coarse, objective sense, means hardly more than a man whom the speaker likes. As a result, gentleman is now a useless word. We had lots of terms of approval already, so it was not needed for that use; on the other hand, if anyone (say, in a historical work) wants to use it in its old sense, he cannot do so without explanations. It has been spoiled for that purpose.

REVISED TEXT:

The word "gentleman" originally had a clear meaning. It referred to someone who had a coat of arms and owned land. When you called someone "a gentleman," you were not complimenting them but stating a fact. If you said someone was not "a gentleman," you were not insulting them but providing information.

12

A gentleman, once it has been spiritualized and refined beyond its original, objective sense, becomes little more than a person the speaker likes. Consequently, "gentleman" is now a meaningless word. We already had plenty of terms for approval, rendering it unnecessary for that purpose. On the other hand, if someone wishes to use it in its original sense (e.g., in a historical work), they would require explanations because the word has lost its significance.

Please note, I have taken *poetic licence* in a few instances to bring clarity to certain of Lewis's arguments. I hope that this does not diminish the essence of his work in any way.

The motivation behind my effort to rework the original manuscript of MERE CHRISTIANITY aligns with what I believe inspired Lewis to write his book in the first place: to help readers discover their ultimate purpose and engage in a personal relationship with the living God.

Despite over seventy years passing since its initial publication, MERE CHRISTIANITY continues to grace the best-seller lists, standing the test of time. It's worth noting that the original text is now in the public domain in some countries.

I received the ultimate compliment when a friend of mine read my book, IF GOD, THEN..., and told me, "I could hear your voice as I was reading it." With that in mind, I'd like to share a link to an original BBC recording[2] featuring C.S. Lewis. Having his voice in the background while reading can be a truly enriching experience.

---

[2] bit.ly/cslewisrecording

If C.S. Lewis and I were able to meet today, I believe we would become fast friends. Both he and I delight in logical arguments, of which Lewis is a master.

Using superscript Roman numerals, I have referenced a few endnotes and afterthoughts.

Enjoy!

C. S. Lewis

C.S. Lewis was an atheist for many years and described his conversion in *Surprised by Joy*: "In the Trinity term of 1929, I gave in and admitted that God was God. Perhaps the most dejected and reluctant convert in all of England." This experience helped him understand not only apathy but also active unwillingness to accept religion. As a Christian writer, Lewis possessed an exceptionally brilliant and logical mind, and his writing style was lucid and lively. He was unrivaled in his works, which include *The Problem of Pain*, *The Screwtape Letters*, *Mere Christianity*, *The Four Loves*, and the posthumous *Prayer: Letters to Malcolm*. In addition to his bestselling works, Lewis also wrote delightful books for children, most notably *The Chronicles of Narnia* series, starting with *The Lion the Witch and the Wardrobe*. He also explored science fiction, along with numerous works of literary criticism. His writings have been translated and read by millions of people worldwide. Lewis passed away on November 22, 1963, at his home in Oxford.

Introduction by C.S. Lewis.

The contents of this book were originally presented on the airwaves and later published in three separate parts: *THE CASE FOR CHRISTIANITY* (1943)[3], *CHRISTIAN BEHAVIOUR* (1943), and *BEYOND PERSONALITY* (1945). While preparing the printed versions, I made a few additions to what I had spoken into the microphone but largely preserved the original text. When delivering a radio talk, I believe it should resemble genuine conversation rather than a recitation of an essay. Therefore, in my talks, I used contractions and colloquialisms that I typically employ in everyday discussions. In the printed edition, I maintained this approach by using "don't" and "we've" instead of "do not" and "we have." Additionally, I italicized words to convey the emphasis I had given them through my voice during the talks.

I now believe that it was a mistake, an undesirable blend of spoken and written art. When speaking, one should use vocal variations for emphasis since the medium naturally lends itself to that method. However, a writer should not rely on italics for the same purpose. A writer has different means of highlighting key words and should utilize them. In this edition, I have expanded contractions and replaced most of the italics by rephrasing the sentences in which they appeared, while preserving the intended "popular" or "familiar" tone. I have also made additions and deletions where I believe I now have a

---

[3] [*] Published in England as Broadcast Talks.

better understanding of certain aspects of my subject compared to ten years ago or where I know that the original version was misunderstood by others.

I must warn the reader that I provide no guidance for those who are undecided between different Christian denominations. I will not advise whether one should become Anglican, Methodist, Presbyterian, or Roman Catholic. This omission is deliberate (even the listing I provided is in alphabetical order). My own position is not mysterious. I am an ordinary layperson[4] of the Church of England, not particularly "high" or "low,"[5] or anything else in particular. However, in this book, I am not attempting to convert anyone to my own position.

Since I became a Christian, I have believed that the best, perhaps the only, service I can offer to my non-believing neighbors is to explain and defend the beliefs that have been common to almost all Christians throughout history. I had more than one reason for this belief. Firstly, the questions that divide Christians often involve matters of deep theology or ecclesiastical history that should only be addressed by true experts. I would be out of my depth in such discussions and would need help myself rather than being able to assist others. Secondly, it seems that discussing these disputed points does not tend to attract outsiders to the Christian faith. As long as we write and talk about these disagreements, we are more likely to discourage them from joining any Christian community rather than drawing them in. Our divisions should only be discussed in the presence of those who have already come to believe in one God and that Jesus Christ is His only Son. Lastly, I had the impression that many more talented authors were already

---

[4] Layperson: a person without professional or specialized knowledge in a particular subject.

[5] anglican.ca/ask/faq/high-low-church/

engaged in such controversial matters rather than defending what Baxter refers to as "mere" Christianity. The area where I believed I could be of greatest service also seemed to be the thinnest. And so, I naturally gravitated towards it.

To the best of my knowledge, these were my only motives, and I would appreciate it if people would not make fanciful assumptions based on my silence regarding certain disputed matters. For instance, such silence does not necessarily mean that I am sitting on the fence. Sometimes I am, as there are questions among Christians to which I do not have the answers. There are even some questions to which I may never know the answer. Even in a better world, if I were to ask them, I might receive a response similar to that given to a greater questioner: "What is that to you? Follow Me."[6] However, there are other questions where I clearly take a position but choose not to express it. I did not write this book to explain "my religion" but to elucidate "mere" Christianity, which is what it is and has been long before my time, whether I like it or not.

Some people may draw unwarranted conclusions from the fact that I do not say more about the Blessed Virgin Mary beyond asserting the Virgin Birth of Christ. However, isn't the reason for this omission obvious? Saying more would immediately plunge me into highly controversial territory. And no controversy among Christians needs to be handled with as much delicacy as this one. Roman Catholic beliefs on this subject are not only fervently held, as with any sincere religious belief, but also defended with a sense of honor and chivalry that one feels when the honor of their mother or beloved is at stake.

---

[6] John 21:22

It is extremely difficult to dissent from these beliefs without appearing not only a heretic[7] but also a cad[8]. Likewise, the opposing Protestant beliefs on this subject stir emotions that touch the very core of Monotheism. Radical Protestants believe that the distinction between the Creator and the creature, no matter how holy, is jeopardized and that Polytheism has resurfaced. Thus, it is challenging to express dissent in a way that does not make one seem worse than a heretic — an idolater, a pagan. If any topic could undermine a book about "mere" Christianity and render it unhelpful to those who do not yet believe that the Virgin's son is God, it is surely this one.

Interestingly, one cannot conclude from my silence on disputed points whether I consider them important or unimportant. That in itself, is a disputed point among Christians. Disagreements arise about the significance of these disagreements. When two Christians of different denominations engage in arguments, it usually doesn't take long for one to question whether such-and-such a point "really matters," and the other responds, "Matter? Why, it's absolutely essential."

I mention all of this to clarify the type of book I have attempted to write, not to conceal or evade responsibility for my own beliefs. As I mentioned earlier, there is no secret about my beliefs. To quote Uncle Toby[9], "They are written in the Common-Prayer Book."

---

[7] Heretic: one whose beliefs or opinions are contrary to orthodox religious (especially Christian) doctrine.

[8] Cad: a man who behaves dishonorably, especially toward a woman.

[9] Uncle Toby is a fictional character created by the Irish author Jonathan Swift in his novel *"Tristram Shandy."* The character of Uncle Toby appears in the book as a kind-hearted and benevolent military officer who is known for his gentle and sentimental nature.

The danger was that I might present as common Christianity something that was specific to the Church of England or, worse yet, specific to myself. To guard against this, I sent the original script of what is now BOOK II to four clergymen (Anglican, Methodist, Presbyterian, Roman Catholic) and requested their criticism. The Methodist felt that I hadn't discussed Faith enough, and the Roman Catholic felt that I had gone too far in downplaying the importance of theories in explaining the Atonement. However, all five of us were in agreement. I did not subject the remaining books to similar scrutiny since any differences would arise among individual Christians or schools of thought rather than between denominations.

Based on reviews and the numerous letters I have received, it seems that the book, despite its flaws, has successfully presented an agreed-upon, common, central, or "mere" Christianity. In this way, it may help dispel the notion that omitting the disputed points leaves only a vague and lifeless H.C.F.[10] The H.C.F. proves to be not only positive but also potent, distinguishing itself from all non-Christian beliefs by a chasm that the worst divisions within Christendom cannot compare to.

While I may not have directly aided the cause of reunion, I have perhaps made it clear why we should seek unity. I have encountered little of the fabled *odium theologicum*[11] from convinced members of different communions. Hostility has mainly come from individuals on the fringes, both within and outside the Church of England, who do not precisely align

---

[10] HCF: Highest Common Factor.

[11] *Odium theologicum:* bitterness developed during or typical of controversy about religion and giving rise to an unyielding refusal to continue a discussion.

themselves with any particular communion[12]. I find this somewhat comforting. It is at the core of each communion, where its most devoted followers reside, that every communion is closest in spirit to every other, if not in doctrine. This suggests that at the center of each communion, there is something — or Someone — who, despite diverging beliefs and temperaments, speaks with the same voice. This covers my omissions on doctrine.

In BOOK III, which deals with morals, I have also chosen not to address certain matters, but for a different reason. Ever since I served as an infantryman in the First World War, I have harbored a strong aversion to those who, safe and comfortable, issue exhortations to those on the front line. As a result, I am reluctant to speak extensively about temptations to which I myself am not exposed. No man is tempted by every sin, and the inclination that drives men to gamble is absent from my nature. Undoubtedly, this deficiency comes at the cost of lacking some virtue associated with it. Therefore, I do not consider myself qualified to offer advice on permissible and impermissible gambling, if there is such a thing, as I do not claim to possess that knowledge. I have also refrained from discussing birth control. I am neither a woman, nor a married man, nor a priest. I did not believe it was my place to take a definitive stance on matters concerning pains, dangers, and expenses that I am shielded from, as I do not hold a pastoral position that would compel me to do so.

Deeper objections may arise — and have been expressed — against my use of the word Christian to denote someone who

---

[12] (In this instance) Communion can describe a sense of sharing, fellowship, or intimate connection with others, often based on common beliefs, experiences, or interests. It signifies a close bond or unity among individuals or a group.

accepts the common doctrines of Christianity. People ask, "Who are you to decide who is and who is not a Christian?" or "Isn't it possible for someone who cannot believe these doctrines to be more truly a Christian, closer to the spirit of Christ, than those who do?" In one sense, this objection is justified, charitable, spiritual, and sensitive. It possesses every admirable quality except usefulness. We simply cannot use language as these objectors propose without disastrous consequences. I will illustrate this with the history of another, much less significant, word.

The word "gentleman" originally had a clear meaning. It referred to someone who had a coat of arms and owned land. When you called someone "a gentleman," you were not complimenting them but stating a fact. If you said someone was not "a gentleman," you were not insulting them but providing information.

It was not contradictory to say that John was a liar and a gentleman, just as it is not contradictory today to say that James is a fool and holds a Master's Degree. However, some people came along—rightly, charitably, spiritually, sensitively—suggesting that the important aspect of being a gentleman is not the coat of arms and land, but rather behavior. They argued that the true gentleman is one who conducts himself in a manner befitting a gentleman. In that sense, Edward is considered far more genuinely a gentleman than John.

Their intentions were good. Honorable, courteous, and brave behavior is undoubtedly superior to owning a coat of arms. However, they are not the same thing. What's more, not everyone agrees on this point. Using the term "gentleman" in this new, refined sense becomes a way of praising someone rather than providing information about them. Denying that someone is "a gentleman" becomes an insult. When a word ceases to describe and becomes solely a term of praise, it no longer conveys factual information about the object; it only reveals the speaker's opinion of that object (e.g., calling a meal "nice"[13] only indicates that the speaker enjoyed it).

A gentleman, once it has been spiritualized and refined beyond its original, objective sense, becomes little more than a person the speaker likes. Consequently, "gentleman" is now a meaningless word. We already had plenty of terms for approval, rendering it unnecessary for that purpose. On the other hand, if someone wishes to use it in its original sense (e.g., in a historical work), they would require explanations because the word has lost its significance.

If we allow people to spiritualize and refine, or as they might say, "deepen," the meaning of the word Christian, it, too, will rapidly become meaningless.

Christians themselves will no longer be able to apply it to anyone. It is not our place to determine who, in the deepest sense, is or is not aligned with the spirit of Christ. We cannot see into people's hearts, and we are forbidden from passing judgment. Using a word that we can never apply effectively renders it useless. Unbelievers, on the other hand, will happily adopt the word in its refined sense as a term of praise. Calling someone a Christian will simply mean that they are deemed a good person. However, this usage adds no value to the language since we already have the word "good."

---

[13] In the late 13c., *nice* meant "foolish, ignorant, frivolous, senseless," from Old French *nice* (12c.) "careless, clumsy; weak; poor, needy; simple, stupid, silly, foolish. By 1926, *nice* was said to be "too great a favorite with the ladies, who have charmed out of it all its individuality and converted it into a mere diffuser of vague and mild agreeableness." [Fowler]

Consequently, the word Christian will have lost any meaningful purpose it might have served.

Therefore, we must adhere to the original, obvious meaning of the word. The term Christians was first used in Antioch (Acts 11:26) to refer to "the disciples," those who accepted the teachings of the apostles. It is not restricted to those who fully embodied those teachings. It is not extended to those who, in a refined, spiritual, inward sense, are "far closer to the spirit of Christ" than some of the less exemplary disciples. This distinction is not a theological or moral one. It simply concerns using words that everyone can understand. When someone who accepts Christian doctrine lives in a manner unworthy of it, it is far clearer to say that they are a bad Christian rather than to deny their Christianity altogether.

I hope no reader assumes that "mere" Christianity is presented here as an alternative to the creeds of existing denominations. It is more akin to a hallway with doors leading to various rooms. If I can guide anyone into that hallway, I will have accomplished my objective. However, it is in the rooms themselves, not the hallway, that one finds warmth, chairs, and meals. The hallway is a place to wait, a place from which to explore the different doors, not a place to settle. In this regard, even the worst room (whichever that may be) is preferable.

It is true that some may find themselves waiting in the hallway for an extended period, while others quickly discern which door they must knock on. I do not know the reason for this discrepancy, but I am certain that God does not keep anyone waiting unless He sees it as beneficial. When you finally enter your room, you will discover that the long wait has conferred some form of good upon you, which you would not have gained otherwise. Nevertheless, you must regard it as waiting, not as setting up camp. Continue to pray for enlightenment, and even in the hallway, begin to abide by the rules that apply throughout the house. Most importantly, inquire as to which door is the true one—not which door pleases you most due to its appearance and decorations.

In simple terms, the question should never be, "Do I like this type of service?" Instead, it should be, "Are these doctrines true? Is holiness present here? Does my conscience draw me towards this? Is my hesitation to knock on this door rooted in pride, personal preference, or a mere dislike of the doorkeeper?"

Once you have reached your own room, be kind to those who have chosen different doors and those who remain in the hallway. If they are mistaken, they need your prayers even more. And if they are your enemies, you are under orders to pray for them. This is one of the rules that applies throughout the entire house.

BOOK I - RIGHT AND WRONG AS A CLUE TO THE MEANING OF THE UNIVERSE

THE LAW OF HUMAN NATURE

E veryone has heard folks quarrelling. Sometimes it sounds funny, sometimes it's simply unpleasant; but regardless of how it sounds, I believe we can glean something quite significant from listening to what they're saying. They'll say things like: "How'd you like it if someone did the same to you?" — "That's my seat, I was here first" — "Leave him be, he's not bothering you" — "Why should you be the first to barge in?" — "Give me a piece of your orange, I gave you a piece of mine" — "Come on, you promised." Every day, people utter such phrases, the educated and the uneducated, children and adults alike. What piques my interest about these remarks is that the individual making them isn't just stating their displeasure with the other's behaviour. They're invoking a certain standard of behaviour that they expect the other to recognise. The other person rarely retorts: "To hell with your standard." They'll usually attempt to argue that their actions don't really contradict the standard, or if they do, there's a special exception. They'll pretend there's a specific reason in this particular instance that the person who nabbed the seat first should not keep it, or that things were completely different when they were handed a piece of orange, or that an unexpected event exempts them from keeping their promise. It appears, in fact, as though both parties are mindful of some sort of Law or Rule concerning fair play, decent behaviour, morality, or whatever else you want to call it, about which they genuinely concur. And they do. If they didn't, they might resort to animalistic fighting, but they wouldn't be able to quarrel in the distinctly human sense. Quarrelling entails attempting to demonstrate that the other person is in the wrong. This endeavour would make no sense unless you and they had some sort of consensus on what constitutes Right and Wrong, just like it would make no sense to claim that a soccer player committed a foul without an agreed-upon set of soccer rules.

The Law or Rule about Right and Wrong used to be referred to as the Law of Nature. Nowadays, when we discuss the "laws of nature", we typically refer to things like gravitation, heredity[14], or chemical laws. But when older thinkers labelled the Law of Right and Wrong "the Law of Nature," they were genuinely referring to the Law of Human Nature. The idea was that, just as all objects are governed by the law of gravitation and living organisms by biological laws, so too is the creature known as man subject to his own law—albeit with one significant difference: a physical body doesn't have a choice whether to obey the law of gravitation or not, but a man or woman can choose either to obey the Law of Human Nature or to flout it.

We can express this in a different way. Every man is constantly subjected to multiple sets of laws, but there's only one of these which he can freely disregard. As a physical body, he's subjected to gravity and cannot defy it; if you leave him unsupported in mid-air, he has as little choice about falling as a stone does. As a living organism, he's subjected to various biological laws, which he can't disobey any more than an animal can. That is to say, he can't disobey those laws which he shares with other entities; but the law unique to his human nature, the law he doesn't share with animals, plants, or inorganic things, is the one he can disobey if he so chooses.

---

[14] genetics

This law was called the Law of Nature because it was believed that everyone knew it by nature and didn't need to be taught it. They didn't mean, of course, that you couldn't find a lone individual here and there who didn't know it, just like you can find a few folks who are colour-blind or have no musical ear. But considering the human race as a whole, they believed that the concept of decent behaviour was evident to everyone. And I reckon they were right. If they weren't, then all the things we've said about the war[15] would be nonsense. What's the point in claiming that the enemy was in the wrong unless Right is a tangible thing, which the Nazis deep down understood as well as we did and should have practiced? If they had no concept of what we mean by right, then, even though we might still have had to fight them, we couldn't have blamed them any more than we could have blamed them for their hair colour.

I'm aware that some folks argue that the idea of a Law of Nature or decent behaviour known to all is unsound because different civilizations and eras have held vastly differing moralities.

But this simply isn't true. There have been disparities in their moral codes, but these have never amounted to anything akin to a total difference. If anyone bothers to compare the moral teachings of, say, the ancient Egyptians, Babylonians, Hindus, Chinese, Greeks, and Romans, what will genuinely strike them is how alike they are to each other and to our own. I've compiled some of the evidence for this in the appendix of another book called THE ABOLITION OF MAN; but for our present purposes, I only need to ask the reader to ponder what a totally different morality would entail. Imagine a country where people are lauded for deserting their comrades in battle, or where a man takes pride in betraying those who have shown him the most

---

[15] Lewis' 'talks' were broadcast during the darkest days of World War Two.

kindness. You might as well try to envision a country where two and two equals five. Men have differed in regards to whom one ought to be unselfish towards—whether it's only your own family, or your fellow countrymen, or everyone. But they've always agreed that you ought not to put yourself first. Selfishness has never been admired. Men have differed as to whether you should have one wife or four. But they've always agreed that you can't simply have any woman you fancy.

But the most remarkable thing is this. Whenever you encounter a man who says he doesn't believe in a real Right and Wrong, you'll find the same man reneging on this statement a moment later. He might break his promise to you, but if you try breaking one to him, he'll be exclaiming "That's not fair!" before you can say Jack Robinson. A nation might proclaim that treaties don't matter, but then, in the next breath, they undermine their argument by declaring that the specific treaty they wish to break was an unfair one. But if treaties don't matter, and if there's no such thing as Right and Wrong—in other words, if there's no Law of Nature—what distinguishes a fair treaty from an unfair one? Haven't they just let the cat out of the bag and demonstrated that, regardless of what they say, they truly understand the Law of Nature just like anyone else?

It seems, then, we're compelled to believe in a real Right and Wrong. People might sometimes err about them, just as folks sometimes make mistakes in their mathematics; but they're not a matter of mere taste and opinion any more than the multiplication table. Now if we can agree on that, I proceed to my next point, which is this: None of us are truly abiding by the Law of Nature. If there are any exceptions among you, I apologize to them. They'd be better off reading some other work, as nothing I'm going to say pertains to them.

And now, addressing the regular folks who are left: I hope you won't misunderstand what I'm about to say. I'm not preaching, and Heaven knows I don't pretend to be better than anyone else. I'm only trying to draw attention to a fact; the fact that this year, or this month, or, more likely, this very day, we've failed to practice ourselves the type of behaviour we expect from others. There may be all sorts of reasons for us. That time you were so unfair to the kids was when you were utterly exhausted. That slightly dodgy business concerning the money — the one you've nearly forgotten — occurred when you were flat broke. And what you vowed to do for old So-and-so and have never done — well, you never would have promised if you'd known how dreadfully busy you were going to be. And as for your behaviour towards your spouse (or partner) or sibling, if I knew how irritating they could be, I wouldn't be surprised — and who the heck am I, anyway? I'm just the same. That is to say, I don't succeed in abiding by the Law of Nature very well, and the instant anyone tells me I'm not following it, a string of excuses as long as your arm springs up in my mind. The question at the moment isn't whether they're valid excuses. The point is that they're yet another testament to how deeply — whether we like it or not — we believe in the Law of Nature. If we didn't believe in decent behaviour, why would we be so eager to make excuses for not having acted decently? The truth is, we believe in decency so much — we feel the Rule or Law pressing on us so — that we can't stand to face the fact that we're breaking it, and consequently we try to shift the blame. Because you'll notice that it's only for our misbehaviour that we devise all these explanations. It's only our bad temper that we attribute to being tired or worried or hungry; we credit our good temper to ourselves.

So, these are the two points I wanted to make. First, that human beings, all over the world, have this peculiar idea that they should behave in a certain way, and can't truly shake it off. Second, that they don't in fact behave in that way. They're aware of the Law of Nature when they break it. These two facts form the foundation of all lucid thinking about ourselves and the universe we inhabit.

SOME OBJECTIONS

If these facts form the foundation, I'd better take a moment to solidify that foundation before moving on. Some of the letters I've received indicate that quite a few people struggle to understand exactly what this Law of Human Nature, or Moral Law, or Rule of Decent Behaviour is.

For instance, some people wrote to me asking, "Isn't what you term the Moral Law simply our herd instinct, and hasn't it evolved just like all our other instincts?" Now, I don't dispute that we might have a herd instinct: but that's not what I'm referring to as the Moral Law. We all know what it feels like to be driven by instinct — by maternal love, or sexual instinct, or the instinct for food. It means that you feel a powerful urge or desire to act in a certain manner. And, of course, we sometimes feel precisely that kind of desire to help another person: and no doubt that desire is attributable to the herd instinct. But feeling a desire to help is quite different from feeling that you should help regardless of whether you want to or not. Suppose you hear a cry for help from a person in danger. You'll most likely feel two opposing desires: one, a desire to provide aid (due to your herd instinct); the other, a desire to keep yourself safe (due to the instinct for self-preservation). But you'll find in yourself, in addition to these two impulses, a third thing which tells you that you should heed the urge to assist and suppress the urge to stay safe. That thing which advises you to do so isn't either of your instincts. It's standing in a higher position, as a judge between them, directing you to obey the one and suppress the other. If it was one of your instincts, you'd be left with only two choices: it couldn't be standing above the fray, directing you to obey one and suppress the other.

In fact, that's the crucial point. The thing that stands above the fray and decides between the instincts, that's what I'm calling the Law of Human Nature or Moral Law. From its vantage point, it decidedly sees some actions as better than others.

Now, of course, I know that the idea of there being anything "higher" than the instincts sounds pretty strange: more so in this present age. But let me endeavour to explain. I'm not denying that instincts exist, or that they can often guide us rightly. But I'm saying that there's a higher authority, something which stands above them and which can, so to speak, pull rank on them. Let's take a real-life example.

Suppose you're placed in charge of a child. And suppose that there's a wasp in the room. You'd have a natural instinct to shoo it away. But your reason tells you that if you do, you'll only be making matters worse—most likely inciting the wasp to sting the child. Therefore, you suppress the instinct to shoo the wasp and let it do its thing, painful as it is to do so. Here, because the safety of the child is a greater value than the comfort of the child, the instinct to protect has to be suppressed. Thus, instincts are merely tendencies or dispositions, each of which is suitable in its proper place, but none of which should guide us indiscriminately. And the thing that decides which instinct should be encouraged in any given circumstance isn't an instinct; it's a rational faculty or conscience or whatever you'd like to call it: a capacity that stands over and regulates the instincts and can distinguish between fulfilling an instinct and indulging it. But this, of course, involves recognizing a distinction between two kinds of reality—namely, between what's in line with the higher or moral law, and what's out of alignment with it, between what's truly right and what merely appears to be or what we would like to be right.

The moment you admit that one instinct can be allowed to override another, that a higher value can be assigned to one course of action and a lower one to another, you are on the road of admitting that there is a real moral law, distinguishable from mere instinct, known to us, and not necessarily known to all animals, a law which constitutes the true measure of right and wrong.

Here is another perspective on the matter: If the Moral Law were simply one of our instincts, we should be able to identify a single impulse within us that always aligns with what we consider "good," consistently adhering to the principles of right behavior. However, this isn't the case. The Moral Law may instruct us to restrain any of our impulses at times and encourage them at others. It's a misconception to label some of our impulses—such as motherly love or patriotism—as inherently good, while regarding others, like sexual desire or the urge to fight, as inherently bad.

What we actually mean is that certain impulses, like the inclination to fight or sexual desire, often require more frequent restraint compared to impulses like motherly love or patriotism. But there are circumstances where it's appropriate for a married man to embrace his sexual desire or for a soldier to embrace his fighting instinct. Similarly, there are occasions when a mother's love for her children or a person's love for their country must be suppressed to prevent unfairness toward others.

Strictly speaking, there are no inherently good or bad impulses. Consider a piano: it doesn't have "right" and "wrong" notes. Each note can be right or wrong depending on the context. The Moral Law isn't tied to any single instinct or set of instincts;

rather, it orchestrates these instincts to create a harmonious tune, what we refer to as goodness or right conduct.

This point holds significant practical implications. The most perilous action is to elevate any single impulse within ourselves as an absolute guide. None of these impulses, if made absolute, would fail to lead us astray. Even seemingly altruistic impulses, like a general love for humanity, can become dangerous if divorced from principles of justice. This can lead individuals to break agreements or manipulate evidence under the guise of serving humanity, ultimately fostering cruelty and treachery.

Some argue that the Moral Law is merely a social construct, instilled in us through education. However, this overlooks a crucial distinction. Just because we learn something from our upbringing doesn't mean it's purely a human invention. Consider the multiplication table: we learn it in school, but its truths are independent of human invention. Similarly, while we learn the principles of decent behavior from various sources, not all of them are mere conventions. Some, like mathematics, represent genuine truths.

The Moral Law belongs in the same category as mathematics for two reasons. Firstly, while moral ideas may vary across time and culture, there's a fundamental similarity underlying them all — a common thread of morality. Conventions, on the other hand, can vary significantly. Secondly, when assessing moralities, we implicitly acknowledge that some are better than others. This implies the existence of a standard against which moralities can be measured — a Real Morality independent of human perception.

In conclusion, despite apparent differences in people's ideas of decent behavior, the very fact that we contemplate these differences suggests the existence of a universal Natural Law of Behavior. However, it's important to note the distinction between differences in morality and differences in beliefs about facts. For instance, the shift away from executing witches isn't a moral advancement but rather a change in factual beliefs about the existence of witches.

The Reality of the Law

Now that we have solidified the idea of the Moral Law or Law of Human Nature, let's turn to the third thing that can be known about it.

One of the notable features of humanity's real moral judgment (as distinct from their mere chatter) is that they regard certain actions as being intrinsically right or wrong.[i] I'm not saying that if we happened to like doing a certain thing, and if doing that thing made us happy, we would naturally come to think it right, and if we disliked it, we would naturally come to think it wrong. I'm not saying that at all. I'm saying that, quite apart from what we feel about it, we can recognize that some things are essentially and objectively right, and others essentially and objectively wrong. We believe that our moral judgments are not mere statements about our feelings, but statements about reality.

This isn't a matter of personal preference. It's a recognition of an external moral law: a law that isn't made by us. It may be imposed on us by others, or it may be a law that we can choose to follow or to disregard. It's a law that doesn't depend on our feelings, but to which our feelings ought to conform.

Now, some people may think this concept of an external moral law is outdated and unfashionable. But I think they're mistaken. Sure, we might have become more skeptical, more doubtful, more inclined to question everything. But the fundamental concept of an external moral law hasn't disappeared. It's simply shifted from being a concept that most people take for granted, to being a concept that's often challenged, debated, and defended.

And despite the skepticism of some, this concept of an external moral law continues to have a tremendous influence on our society. It's the basis for our legal system, for our notions of justice and fairness, for our beliefs about human rights, and for many of our most deeply held values. Even when we disagree about the specifics of what's right and wrong, we still agree on the principle that there is such a thing as right and wrong, and that this isn't just a matter of opinion or personal preference.

WHAT LIES BEHIND THE LAW

Let's summarize what we have discussed so far. When it comes to objects like stones and trees, the so-called Laws of Nature may simply be a way of describing their observed behavior. These laws may not be anything substantial or beyond the observed facts. However, in the case of human beings, this explanation is insufficient. The Law of Human Nature, or the concept of Right and Wrong, must transcend mere observations of human behavior. It represents a genuine law that exists independently and obliges us to abide by it.

Now, let's consider what this tells us about the universe we inhabit. Throughout history, people have pondered the nature of the universe and its origin. Broadly speaking, two perspectives have emerged. The first is the materialist view, which suggests that matter and space exist by chance and have always existed, without any discernible purpose. According to this view, matter, following certain fixed patterns, happened to give rise to creatures like us who possess the ability to think. It's a series of fortunate events that led to the formation of our solar system, the emergence of life-sustaining conditions on Earth, and the subsequent development of living organisms. The second perspective is the religious view. It posits that the essence behind the universe resembles a mind rather than any known entity.

Please note that these two views have coexisted throughout history. Furthermore, it's important to recognize that science, in its conventional sense, cannot definitively answer the question regarding the existence of something beyond the observed facts. Science operates through experimentation and observation of behavior. Every scientific statement ultimately boils down to something like, "I observed this particular phenomenon at a specific time and place." The realm beyond observed facts, whether in the case of stones, weather, or the universe itself, cannot be elucidated through external study.

However, there is one aspect of the universe that we know more about than we can learn through external observation alone, and that is humanity. We not only observe human behavior, but we also possess an intrinsic understanding because we are human ourselves. In this case, we have access to "inside information"; we are familiar with the subject matter. And based on our introspection, we find that human beings are bound by a moral law, which is not of their own making, and which they cannot completely ignore, even when they try. It is a law that compels us to do what is right and makes us feel responsible and uneasy when we do wrong.

Consider the following point: if someone were to study humans from an external perspective, lacking our language and the ability to gain inside knowledge from us, they would never find evidence of this moral law. How could they? Their observations would merely reveal what we do, while the moral law pertains to what we ought to do. Similarly, if there were something transcendent or foundational behind the observed facts of stones or the weather, studying them from an external standpoint would never lead to its discovery.

The situation can be described as follows: we desire to understand whether the universe exists for a reason or if it simply happened without any purpose. Since this reason, if it exists, would not be among the observed facts but a reality that underlies them, mere observation cannot reveal it. There is only one case in which we can acquire knowledge about it, and that is our own case as humans. And within that context, we find that there is indeed something more. Or to put it differently, if there were a controlling power beyond the universe, it could not manifest itself as one of the facts within the universe. It would be akin to an architect being identified as a wall, staircase, or fireplace within the house they designed. The only way we could expect such a power to manifest itself would be from within, as an influence or command that strives to guide our behavior in a certain way. And that is precisely what we find within ourselves.

It is important to note that I am not making claims about the God of Christian theology at this stage. I have only established the existence of a directing force within the universe, which manifests in me as a law that urges me to do what is right and makes me feel responsible and uncomfortable when I do wrong. I believe we should consider this force to be more akin to a mind than anything else we know, as it is challenging to imagine an inanimate object giving instructions. However, it need not resemble a mind or a person precisely. In the next chapter, we will delve deeper into this topic. Nevertheless, I must issue a word of caution. For the past century, there has been a great deal of misleading rhetoric about God. I am not offering that kind of soft-spoken discourse. You can discard all of that.

Note: In order to condense this section for the radio broadcast, I only mentioned the Materialist and Religious views. However, for completeness, I should mention the intermediary viewpoint known as Life-Force philosophy, Creative Evolution, or Emergent Evolution. This perspective suggests that the variations leading from the lowest life forms to humans were not random but driven by a striving or purposefulness within a Life-Force. When people espouse this view, we must question whether they consider the Life-Force to possess a mind. If they do, then "a mind bringing life into existence and guiding its progression" is essentially God, rendering their view equivalent to the Religious perspective. If they do not attribute a mind to it, then the notion of something without a mind striving or having purposes becomes nonsensical, thereby undermining their viewpoint. Many people find Creative Evolution appealing because it offers emotional comfort akin to belief in God without the less pleasant consequences. When you feel vibrant and the sun is shining, and you prefer not to believe that the universe is a mere mechanical dance of atoms, it's comforting to think of a mysterious force propelling you forward throughout the centuries. Conversely, when you contemplate engaging in less virtuous actions, the Life-Force, being a blind force devoid of morals or a mind, will not hinder you like the troublesome God you learned about in childhood. The Life-Force can be regarded as a tamed version of God. You can switch it on when you desire, but it will not inconvenience you. It provides all the thrills of religion without any associated costs. Is the Life-Force the ultimate embodiment of wishful thinking?

WE HAVE CAUSE TO BE UNEASY

In the previous chapter, I suggested that there is someone or something beyond the material universe that is concerned with our adherence to the Moral Law. Some of you may have felt annoyed or deceived, thinking that I had led you into a religious discussion disguised as philosophy. But let me address those concerns.

Firstly, regarding the idea of putting the clock back, consider this: would you think it's a joke if I said that you can put the hands of a clock back and that it's often a sensible thing to do if the clock is wrong? Let's move away from that metaphor, though. Progress means moving closer to where you want to be. If you've taken a wrong turn, continuing forward won't bring you any closer. Progress, in that case, means turning around and retracing your steps to get on the right path[ii]. The most progressive person is the one who turns back the soonest. We've all experienced this in mathematics. When we start a calculation the wrong way, the sooner we admit it and start over, the faster we progress. There's nothing progressive about being stubborn and refusing to admit a mistake. If we look at the state of the world today, it's evident that humanity has made significant errors. We are on the wrong road, and if that's the case, we must go back. Going back is the quickest way forward.

Secondly, this discussion hasn't yet become a religious discourse. We haven't reached the God of any particular religion, let alone Christianity. We have only arrived at the concept of a Somebody or Something behind the Moral Law.

We're not relying on the Bible or the Church; we are attempting to explore this Somebody using our own intellectual efforts. What we discover through this process is something that surprises us. We have two pieces of evidence about this Somebody. The first is the universe itself, which He has created. If we were to use this as our only clue, we might conclude that He is a great artist because the universe is beautiful. However, it would also suggest that He is merciless and not a friend to humanity, as the universe is dangerous and terrifying. The second piece of evidence is the Moral Law that He has implanted in our minds. This is more reliable evidence because it is an internal experience. We learn more about God through the Moral Law than from the universe as a whole, just as we learn more about a person by listening to their words rather than examining a house they have built. Based on this second piece of evidence, we can deduce that the Being behind the universe is deeply concerned with right conduct - fairness, unselfishness, courage, good faith, honesty, and truthfulness. In that sense, we agree with Christianity and other religions that God is "good." However, let's not rush to conclusions. The Moral Law does not provide grounds for thinking that God is "good" in terms of being indulgent, lenient, or sympathetic. The Moral Law is unforgiving; it tells us to do what is right regardless of how painful, dangerous, or difficult it may be. If God is like the Moral Law, then He is not soft.

At this stage, it's pointless to define a "good" God as one who can forgive. Only a person can forgive, and we haven't reached the stage of a personal God yet. We have only arrived at a power, akin to a mind, behind the Moral Law. However, it's possible that this power is very unlike a person. If it is purely impersonal, then there is no point in asking it to make allowances or forgive, just as there is no point in asking the multiplication table to overlook our errors. We would inevitably

46

arrive at the wrong answer. It's also futile to say that if such an impersonal absolute goodness exists, you don't like it and won't bother about it. The trouble is that a part of you is on the side of absolute goodness and agrees with its disapproval of human greed, trickery, and exploitation. You may want an exception made in your case, but deep down, you know that unless the power behind the world genuinely detests such behavior, it cannot be considered good. On the other hand, we know that if absolute goodness exists, it must despise much of what we do. This puts us in a terrible predicament.

If the universe is not governed by absolute goodness, then all our efforts are ultimately hopeless. But if it is, then we make ourselves enemies of that goodness every day, and there's little chance of improvement in the future. We cannot do without absolute goodness, yet we cannot do well with it either. God is our only source of comfort, but He is also the supreme terror. He is both our greatest need and the thing we most want to hide from. He is our only potential ally, yet we have made ourselves His enemies. Some people speak as if meeting the gaze of absolute goodness would be enjoyable, but they need to reconsider. They are still playing with religion. Goodness can be either the greatest safety or the greatest danger, depending on how we respond to it. Unfortunately, we have reacted in the wrong way.

Now, onto my third point. The reason I took this roundabout approach to reach my real subject was not to trick or deceive you. I had a different intention. My aim was to highlight that Christianity only makes sense when we confront the kind of facts I've been describing. Christianity calls people to repentance[ii] and promises forgiveness. Therefore, it has nothing to offer (as far as I know) to those who are unaware of any wrongdoing or do not feel the need for forgiveness. Christianity's message resonates when we acknowledge the existence of a genuine Moral Law, recognize the power behind it, and understand that we have violated that law and placed ourselves at odds with that Power. Only then, and not a moment sooner, does Christianity become relevant. When you know you are sick, you will listen to the doctor. Likewise, when you realize that our situation is almost desperate, you will begin to comprehend what Christians are talking about. They provide an explanation of how we ended up hating goodness and yet desiring it. They offer insights into how God can be the impersonal mind behind the Moral Law while also being a person. They explain how the demands of the law, which neither you nor I can fulfill, have been met on our behalf, and how God Himself becomes a man to save humanity from God's disapproval. It's an old story, and if you wish to explore it further, consult those who have more authority on the matter than I do. All I'm doing is asking people to face the facts and understand the questions that Christianity claims to answer. These facts are terrifying, and I wish I could offer something more agreeable. However, I must express what I believe to be true. Certainly, the Christian religion provides unimaginable comfort in the long run, but it doesn't begin with comfort; it starts with the dismay I have described. It's futile to seek comfort without first experiencing that dismay.

In religion, just like in war or anything else, comfort cannot be obtained by actively seeking it. If you seek truth, you may ultimately find comfort. But if you seek comfort alone, you will find neither comfort nor truth. Instead, you'll encounter empty rhetoric and wishful thinking at first, followed by despair. Many of us have grown out of our pre-war wishful thinking about international politics, and it's time we do the same with religion.

BOOK II
WHAT CHRISTIANS BELIEVE

THE RIVAL CONCEPTIONS OF GOD

D ifferent Views of God. I've been asked to explain what Christians believe, and I want to start by clarifying one thing that Christians don't necessarily have to believe. If you're a Christian, it doesn't mean you have to believe that all other religions are completely wrong. If you're an atheist, however, you do have to believe that all religions in the world are fundamentally mistaken. As a Christian, you are free to think that other religions, even the strangest ones, contain at least some element of truth. When I was an atheist, I had to convince myself that the majority of humanity had always been wrong about the most important question in their lives. But when I became a Christian, I adopted a more open-minded perspective. However, being a Christian does mean recognizing that Christianity is right and other religions are wrong in areas where they differ. It's similar to mathematics — there is only one correct answer to a math problem, and all other answers are incorrect, though some might be closer to being right than others.

The first major division among people is between the majority who believe in some form of God or gods and the minority who do not. On this point, Christianity aligns with the majority, which includes ancient Greeks and Romans, modern indigenous peoples, Stoics, Platonists, Hindus, Muslims, and others, against the modern Western European materialists.

Now, let's move on to the next significant division. Among those who believe in God, there are different ideas about the nature of God. Two distinct concepts exist in this regard. One idea is that God is beyond good and evil. As humans, we differentiate between good and bad. However, according to some, this is merely a human perspective. These individuals argue that the wiser one becomes, the less inclined they are to label things as good or bad. They believe that as wisdom grows, one realizes that everything has both positive and negative aspects and that nothing could have been different. Consequently, they think that long before reaching the divine perspective, the distinction between good and evil would disappear entirely. For example, they might say we consider cancer bad because it kills a person, but one could also consider a skilled doctor bad because they kill cancer. It all depends on one's point of view. The other and opposing idea is that God is unquestionably "good" or "righteous." This is a God who takes sides, who loves love and hates hatred, and who expects certain behaviors from us. The first view, which believes God is beyond good and evil, is called Pantheism. It was held by the prominent Prussian philosopher Hegel and, as far as I understand, by Hindus. The other view is held by Jews, Muslims, and Christians.

Alongside this major difference between Pantheism and the Christian concept of God, there is often another distinction. Pantheists usually believe that God, in a manner of speaking, animates the universe, just as you animate your body. They see the universe as almost being God, so that if the universe didn't exist, God wouldn't exist either. According to them, everything we find in the universe is part of God. In contrast, the Christian idea is quite different. Christians believe that God created and crafted the universe, much like a person creating a painting or composing a song. A painter is not the painting, and the painter doesn't cease to exist if the painting is destroyed. One might say that the painter has put a significant part of themselves into the artwork, but this merely means that its beauty and interest originated from their mind. The painter's skill is not in the painting in the same way it is in their mind or hands. Hopefully, you can see how this distinction between Pantheists and Christians connects with the previous difference. If you don't take the distinction between good and evil too seriously, it's easy to say that everything in the world is part of God. However, if you genuinely believe some things are truly bad and God is genuinely good, you cannot speak like that. You must believe that God is separate from the world, and some of the things we encounter in it go against His will. When faced with a cancer or a slum, a Pantheist might say, "If you could see it from the divine perspective, you would realize that this too is God." The Christian response would be, "Don't talk nonsense."

Please note: One listener complained about the word "damned" as frivolous swearing. But I mean exactly what I say — nonsense that is damned is under God's curse and will, unless granted divine grace, lead those who believe in it to eternal death.

Christianity is, in essence, a fighting religion. It holds that God created the world — that space and time, heat and cold, all colors and tastes, and every living creature and plant are things that God created, similar to how a person invents a story. However, Christianity also believes that many things have gone awry in the world God created, and God insists, emphatically, that we set things right again.

This raises a significant question: If a good God made the world, why has it gone wrong? For many years, I stubbornly refused to listen to the Christian answers to this question because I kept thinking, "Regardless of what you say, and no matter how clever your arguments may be, isn't it simpler and easier to say that the world wasn't created by an intelligent power? Aren't all your arguments just a convoluted attempt to avoid the obvious?" However, this led me into another predicament.

My argument against God was rooted in the perception that the universe appeared so cruel and unjust. But where did I get the concept of justice and injustice? A person doesn't consider a line crooked unless they have an idea of a straight line. So, when I called the universe unjust, what was I comparing it to? If the entire existence was bad and devoid of meaning from beginning to end, so to speak, why did I, who was supposed to be part of this existence, react so strongly against it? A person feels wet when they fall into water because humans aren't aquatic creatures. A fish wouldn't feel wet.

Of course, I could have abandoned my idea of justice by declaring it a mere personal notion. However, if I did that, my argument against God would also collapse. After all, my argument rested on the assumption that the world was genuinely unjust, not simply that it failed to align with my personal preferences. Hence, in my attempt to prove that God didn't exist—in other words, that reality was entirely senseless—I found myself compelled to assume that one aspect of reality—namely, my concept of justice—actually had meaning.

Therefore, atheism turns out to be too simplistic. If the entire universe lacks purpose, we would never have discovered that it lacks purpose. Just as we wouldn't know it was dark if there were no light in the universe and, consequently, no creatures with eyes. Darkness would be devoid of meaning.

THE INVASION

Alright then, atheism is too simplistic. Now let me tell you about another viewpoint that is also too simplistic. It's what I call "Christianity-and-water," a view that simply states there is a good God in Heaven and everything is fine. This perspective conveniently leaves out all the challenging and troubling doctrines about sin, hell, the devil, and redemption. Both of these views are like children's philosophies.

Asking for a simple religion is futile because real things are not simple. They may appear simple, but they are not. For instance, the table I'm sitting at may look simple, but when you ask a scientist to explain its composition—about atoms, light waves, how they reach my eyes, and their impact on the optic nerve and brain—you'll find that what we call "seeing a table" leads to mysteries and complexities that are hard to comprehend. Similarly, a child saying a prayer seems simple, and if you're content with that, then that's fine. But if you want to delve deeper and understand what is truly happening, be prepared for something more intricate. If we desire more than simplicity, it's foolish to complain that the additional complexity is lacking simplicity.

Often, however, this foolish approach is adopted by people who are not foolish themselves but consciously or unconsciously want to undermine Christianity. They present a version of Christianity suitable for a six-year-old child and use that as their target. When you attempt to explain the actual Christian doctrine as understood by an informed adult, they complain that it's too confusing and complicated. They argue that if there truly were a God, He would have made "religion" simple because simplicity is beautiful. Be cautious of such individuals because they change their arguments constantly and only waste your time. Furthermore, notice their idea of God "making religion simple" as if "religion" were something God invented, rather than His communication to us about certain unchangeable facts concerning His own nature.

In addition to being complex, reality, in my experience, is usually peculiar. It's not tidy, obvious, or as expected. For example, once you understand that the Earth and other planets orbit the sun, you might naturally expect that all the planets would be perfectly matched—equally distant from each other, or distances that consistently increase, or all the same size, or perhaps becoming larger or smaller as you move farther from the sun. But in reality, there seems to be no rhyme or reason (at least none that we can discern) regarding the sizes or distances of the planets. Moreover, some have one moon, one has four, one has two, some have none, and one even has a ring[16].

Indeed, reality is often something you couldn't have predicted. That's one of the reasons why I believe in Christianity. It is a religion that couldn't have been concocted by human imagination. If it offered us exactly the type of universe we had always expected, I would suspect we were inventing it ourselves. However, it's not the sort of thing anyone would have imagined. It has that peculiar twist that real things possess. So, let's leave behind these childish philosophies and simplistic

---

[16] Since C.S. Lewis made this reference to our solar system's planets, the latest count is: One moon for Earth; two for Mars; 95 at Jupiter; 146 at Saturn; 27 at Uranus; 14 at Neptune; and five for dwarf planet Pluto. solarsystem.nasa.gov/moons/overview/

answers. The problem we face is not simple, and the solution won't be simpler either.

Now, what is the problem? We find ourselves in a universe that contains much that is evidently bad and seemingly meaningless. Yet, we, as creatures, understand that it is bad and lacks meaning. Only two views confront all the facts. One is the Christian view that this is a good world that has gone astray but still retains the memory of what it should have been. The other view is called Dualism. Dualism holds that there are two equal and independent powers behind everything — one good and the other bad — and this universe is the battleground where they endlessly fight. Personally, I believe that next to Christianity, Dualism is the most reasonable and courageous creed available. However, it has a flaw.

According to Dualism, the two powers or spirits — the good one and the bad one — are assumed to be completely independent. They both have existed from eternity. Neither of them created the other, and neither has any more right than the other to be called God. Each believes it is good and regards the other as bad. One favors hatred and cruelty, while the other prefers love and mercy, with each backing its own perspective. Now, what do we mean when we label one of them the Good Power and the other the Bad Power? Either we are merely expressing our preference for one over the other, like preferring beer to apple juice, or we are stating that, regardless of what the two powers think or what we humans currently favor, one of them is objectively wrong in considering itself good. If we mean that we simply prefer the first, then we must abandon discussing good and evil altogether. After all, good means what we should prefer, regardless of our momentary likes. If "being good" simply meant aligning with our fleeting preferences without any genuine reason, then goodness wouldn't deserve to be called good. Therefore, we must imply that one of the two powers is truly wrong, while the other is genuinely right.

However, the moment we assert that, we introduce into the universe a third element in addition to the two powers — an objective law, standard, or rule of good that one power adheres to while the other fails to follow. Since both powers are evaluated based on this standard, it means this standard, or the Being who established it, stands above and beyond both powers. This Being becomes the true God. In essence, what we initially referred to as good and bad turns out to mean that one power maintains a correct relationship with the ultimate God, while the other has an incorrect relationship with Him.

We can illustrate this point differently. If Dualism were true, then the bad Power must be a being who derives pleasure from badness itself. However, in reality, we have no experience of anyone enjoying badness solely because it is bad. The closest approximation is found in cruelty. But in real life, people are cruel for one of two reasons: either they are sadists, meaning they have a sexual perversion that derives sensual pleasure from cruelty, or they are cruel for the sake of gaining something — money, power, or safety. Pleasure, money, power, and safety are all, to some extent, good things. The badness lies in pursuing them through improper means, in the wrong manner, or excessively. Of course, I don't mean to imply that people who act this way are not wicked. I simply mean that wickedness, upon closer examination, turns out to be the pursuit of some good in an improper manner. You can be good purely for the sake of goodness itself, but you cannot be bad solely for the sake of badness. You can perform a kind act even when you don't feel kind or derive pleasure from it, simply because kindness is right. However, nobody commits a cruel act purely because cruelty is wrong; they do so because cruelty brings them pleasure or serves some utility. In other words, badness cannot truly succeed in being bad in the same way that goodness succeeds in being good. Goodness exists as an inherent quality, whereas badness is merely goodness spoiled. And for something to be spoiled, there must have been something good in the first place. We describe sadism as a sexual perversion, but you must first have the notion of normal sexuality before you can talk about its perversion. And you can identify the perversion because you can explain the perverted through the normal, but you cannot explain the normal through the perverted. Consequently, this Bad Power, who is presumed to be on equal footing with the Good Power and loves badness just as the Good Power loves goodness, is nothing more than a mere illusion. In order to be bad, this Power must have good things to desire and subsequently corrupt, which means it must possess impulses that were originally good to pervert. However, if this Power is truly bad, it cannot generate good desires or possess good impulses. It must acquire both from the Good Power. Therefore, it is not independent but rather a part of the Good Power's world. It was either created by the Good Power or by a higher power above them both.

To put it even more simply, to be bad, this Power must exist and possess intelligence and will. However, existence, intelligence, and will are inherently good. Therefore, this Power must acquire them from the Good Power. Even in being bad, it must borrow or steal from its opponent. And now you can understand why Christianity has always claimed that the devil is a fallen angel. This is not merely a children's tale; it is a recognition that evil is a parasite, not an original entity. The powers that enable evil to persist are powers bestowed upon it by goodness. All the things that allow a wicked person to effectively carry out their wickedness are, in themselves, good things—determination, cleverness, physical attractiveness, and existence itself. That's why Dualism, strictly speaking, doesn't hold up.

However, I must admit that genuine Christianity (as opposed to diluted versions) aligns more closely with Dualism than people realize. When I first read the New Testament carefully, one thing that surprised me was its extensive mention of a Dark Power in the universe — a mighty evil spirit who was considered to be the force behind death, disease, and sin. The difference lies in Christianity's belief that this Dark Power was created by God and was initially good but went astray. Christianity agrees with Dualism that this universe is in conflict, but it does not perceive it as a war between independent powers. Instead, it views it as a civil war, a rebellion. We are currently residing in a region of the universe occupied by the rebel.

Think of it as enemy-occupied territory — this is what the world is. Christianity tells the story of how the rightful king, in a way, has landed on this territory in disguise and is summoning all of us to join a grand campaign of sabotage. When you attend church, you are essentially eavesdropping on the secret wireless transmissions from our allies. That's why the enemy is so eager to prevent us from going. The enemy accomplishes this by exploiting our vanity, laziness, and intellectual snobbery. Someone will likely ask, "Do you really mean, in this day and age, to reintroduce our old friend, the devil, complete with hooves and horns?" Well, I don't understand what the current time has to do with it. As for the hooves and horns, I'm not fixated on those details. However, in other aspects, my answer is yes, I do believe in the devil. I don't claim to know anything about his physical appearance. If someone genuinely wants to know him better, I would say to that person, "Don't worry. If you genuinely want to, you will. Whether you'll like it when you do is another question."

THE SHOCKING ALTERNATIVE

So, Christians believe that there is an evil power who has taken control of the world for now. This raises some questions. Is this situation according to God's plan? If it is, then God seems strange. And if it isn't, how can anything happen against the will of a supremely powerful being?

Well, anyone in a position of authority knows that something can align with their will in one way but not in another. For example, a mother might tell her children, "I won't tidy up your bedroom for you every night. You have to learn to keep it tidy on your own." Then, one night, she goes upstairs and finds toys, ink, and textbooks scattered everywhere. That goes against her will. She would prefer the children to be tidy. However, her will allowed the children to have the freedom to be messy. The same thing happens in other areas of life, such as in an infantry regiment, trade union, or school. When something is made voluntary, not everyone will participate. That may not be what was willed, but the will itself made it possible.

Likewise, in the universe, God created beings with free will. This means they can choose to do right or wrong. Some people may think it's possible to imagine a creature that is free but incapable of doing wrong, but I cannot. If something is free to do good, it is also free to do evil. And it is this free will that has made evil possible. So why did God give them free will? Because although free will allows for the possibility of evil, it is also the only way to have true love, goodness, and joy. A world filled with beings who simply functioned like machines would not be worth creating. The happiness that God intends for His higher creatures is the happiness of being freely and willingly united with Him and with each other in a love and delight that surpasses even the most intense human love between a man and a woman. And for that to happen, freedom is necessary.

Of course, God knew what would happen if they misused their freedom. Yet, apparently, He considered it worth the risk. We might feel inclined to disagree with Him, but there's a difficulty in doing so. God is the source of our reasoning power. We couldn't be right while He is wrong, just as a stream cannot flow higher than its source. When we argue against God, we are essentially arguing against the very power that allows us to argue in the first place. It's like cutting off the branch we're sitting on. If God believes that this state of conflict in the universe is a price worth paying for free will, for creating a living world where creatures can genuinely do good or harm and where things of real importance can occur, instead of a world that simply operates as a toy moved by God's commands, then we can assume it is indeed worth paying.

Once we understand the concept of free will, we will realize how foolish it is to ask why God created a creature made of such flawed material that it would go astray. The better the material a creature is made of — its intelligence, strength, and freedom — the better it will be if it chooses rightly, but also the worse it will be if it chooses wrongly. A cow cannot be very good or very bad; a dog can be both better and worse; a child can be even better or worse; an ordinary man, even more so; a person of exceptional talent, even more so; and a superhuman spirit, best or worst of all.

How did the Dark Power go wrong? That's a question to which humans cannot provide a definite answer. However, based on our own experiences of going astray, we can make a reasonable guess. The moment we have a self, there is the possibility of putting ourselves first, wanting to be the center, wanting to be God in a sense. That was the sin of Satan, and it's the sin he passed on to the human race. Some people mistakenly believe that the fall of humanity had something to do with sex, but that's not the case. The story in the Book of Genesis suggests that some corruption in our sexual nature followed the fall and was a result of it, not the cause. What Satan implanted in our distant ancestors was the idea that they could "be like gods," establishing themselves as if they had created themselves, being their own masters, and finding happiness apart from God, independent of Him. And from that futile attempt, nearly all of what we call human history has emerged — money, poverty, ambition, war, prostitution, social classes, empires, slavery — the long and painful story of humans seeking something other than God that would bring them happiness.

The reason why this pursuit can never succeed is simple. God created us, just as an inventor designs an engine. A car is designed to run on gasoline, and it won't function properly with any other fuel. Similarly, God designed the human spirit to run on Himself. He Himself is the source of energy our spirits were intended to burn, the nourishment our spirits were meant to feed on. There is no alternative. That's why it's futile to ask God to make us happy in our own way without considering religion. God cannot give us happiness and peace separate from Himself because it simply does not exist. There is no such thing.

This understanding is the key to understanding history. Tremendous efforts have been made, civilizations have been built, and excellent institutions have been created. But every time, something goes wrong. Some fatal flaw always elevates selfish and cruel individuals to power, and everything falls back into misery and ruin. Essentially, the machine breaks down. It may seem to start well and run for a short while, but then it malfunctions. People are trying to run it on the wrong fuel. That's what Satan has done to us humans.

So, what did God do? First, He gave us conscience, the sense of right and wrong. Throughout history, there have been people who have tried, some with great effort, to follow their conscience. However, none of them have fully succeeded. Second, He sent humanity what I refer to as "good dreams," meaning those strange stories found in various pagan religions about a god who dies and resurrects, bringing new life to humanity through his death. And third, He chose a specific group of people, the Jews, and spent centuries instilling in them the understanding of what kind of God He is — that there is only one God and that He cares about righteous conduct. The account of this process can be found in the Old Testament.

Now comes the truly astonishing part. Among the Jews, a man suddenly appeared who spoke as if He were God. He claimed the power to forgive sins, declared His eternal existence, and announced that He would judge the world in the future. Let's make this clear. Among polytheistic belief systems, like Hinduism, anyone could claim to be a part of God or one with God, and it wouldn't be particularly surprising. But because this man was a Jew, He couldn't mean that kind of God. In their language, God referred to the Being outside the world who created it and was entirely different from anything else. And when we grasp this, we realize that what this man said was, without a doubt, the most shocking statement ever uttered by a human being.

One part of His claim often slips by unnoticed because we've heard it so many times that we don't fully understand its significance. I'm referring to His claim to forgive sins, any sins. Unless the speaker is God, this claim is utterly absurd and borders on comedy. We can all comprehend how a person forgives offenses committed against them. If you accidentally step on my foot, I can forgive you. If you steal my money, I can forgive you. But what should we make of a person, who hasn't been wronged or harmed, announcing that they forgive you for stepping on other people's toes and stealing other people's money? It would be a ridiculously nonsensical and conceited statement. Yet, this is exactly what Jesus did. He told people that their sins were forgiven, without waiting to consult all the other people who were undoubtedly affected by those sins. He acted as if He were the primary party involved, the one most offended in every transgression. This only makes sense if He truly was the God whose laws are broken and whose love is wounded in every sin. If these words were spoken by anyone other than God, they would imply a level of foolishness and conceit unmatched by any other figure in history.

However, even His enemies, when reading the Gospels, do not usually perceive Him as foolish or conceited. And unbiased readers certainly do not. Jesus claims to be "humble and meek," and we believe Him, not realizing that if He were merely a man, humility and meekness would be the last characteristics we could attribute to some of His statements.

I'm trying to prevent anyone from saying the truly foolish thing that people often say about Jesus: "I accept Him as a great moral teacher, but I don't accept His claim to be God." That is the one thing we must not say. If Jesus were merely a human being and said the things He said, He wouldn't be a great moral teacher. He would either be a lunatic, on the same level as someone who claims to be a poached egg, or He would be the Devil himself. You must make a choice. Either this man was and is the Son of God, or He was a madman or something even worse. You can dismiss Him as a fool, spit at Him, and kill Him as if He were a demon. Alternatively, you can fall at His feet and acknowledge Him as Lord and God. But let's not indulge in patronizing nonsense by considering Him a great human teacher. He did not leave that option open to us, and it was not His intention to do so.

THE PERFECT PENITENT

Now we are faced with a terrifying alternative. Either this man we're talking about was exactly who He claimed to be, or He was a lunatic or something worse. It seems obvious to me that He was neither a lunatic nor a fiend. Therefore, however strange or frightening or unlikely it may seem, I have to accept the view that He was and is God. God came to this world occupied by the enemy in human form.

Now, what was the purpose of it all? What did He come to do? Well, to teach, of course. But when we delve into the New Testament or any other Christian writings, we find that they constantly emphasize something different — His death and resurrection. It's clear that Christians consider this to be the focal point of the story. They believe that the main reason He came to Earth was to suffer and be killed.

Before I became a Christian, I thought that the first thing Christians had to believe was a specific theory about the purpose of His death. According to that theory, God wanted to punish humanity for deserting Him and joining the Great Rebel. However, Christ volunteered to be punished in our place, so God let us off. Although I now see that this theory is not as immoral or silly as I once thought, it's not the point I want to make. Later on, I realized that this theory or any other is not Christianity itself. The central belief of Christianity is that Christ's death somehow reconciled us with God and gave us a fresh start. Theories on how it accomplished this are secondary. Many different theories have been proposed, and Christians don't all agree on them. My own church, the Church of England, doesn't assert any specific theory as the correct one. The Roman Catholic Church goes further, but they would also agree that the actual event is much more important than any theological explanations. They would probably admit that no explanation will ever fully capture the reality. I'm just a layperson, and we're venturing into deep waters at this point. I can only share my personal perspective on the matter.

In my view, the theories themselves aren't the core of what you're asked to accept. You may have read books by James Jeans or Arthur Eddington, and when they want to explain something like the atom, they provide a description that helps you form a mental picture. But they caution that the picture is not what scientists actually believe. Scientists believe in a mathematical formula. The pictures are there only to assist you in understanding the formula. They're not inherently true like the formula itself; they're just approximations. They are meant to help, but if they don't, you can discard them. The thing itself, however, cannot be pictured; it can only be expressed mathematically. We're in a similar situation here. We believe that Christ's death is the point in history where something utterly unimaginable from outside our world breaks through into our reality. And if we can't even picture the atoms that make up our world, it's impossible for us to picture this event. In fact, if we could fully understand it, that would show it's not what it claims to be—the inconceivable, the uncreated, something beyond nature that penetrates nature like lightning. You might wonder what good it does us if we don't understand it. The answer is simple: A person can eat a meal without understanding precisely how it nourishes them. Similarly, we can accept what Christ has done without fully grasping how it works. In fact, we won't truly understand how it works until we accept it.

We're told that Christ was killed for us, that His death has washed away our sins, and that through His death, He has defeated death itself. That's the essence of it. That's Christianity. That's what needs to be believed. The various theories about how Christ's death achieved all this are, in my view, secondary explanations about the mechanics of it. Christians may not all agree on how important these theories are. The Church of England, for example, doesn't single out one theory as the correct one. The Church of Rome takes a stronger stance. Nonetheless, they all agree that the event itself is far more significant than any explanations theologians have devised. They would likely acknowledge that no explanation can fully capture the reality. But as I mentioned in the preface of this book, I'm just an ordinary person, and we're entering deep waters here. I can only share how I personally perceive the matter.

The most common theory that people have heard is the one I mentioned earlier — the idea that we are forgiven because Christ volunteered to bear the punishment in our place. At first glance, this theory seems absurd. If God was willing to forgive us, why didn't He simply do so? What's the point of punishing an innocent person instead? I don't see any reason for it if we understand punishment in the sense of a court proceeding. However, if we think of it as a debt, then it makes sense for someone who has assets to pay it on behalf of someone who doesn't. Similarly, if we understand "paying the penalty" not as punishment but as "taking responsibility" or "settling the bill," we recognize that when someone gets into trouble, a kind friend often steps in to help them out. So, what kind of "trouble" had humanity gotten itself into? We had tried to assert our independence, to behave as if we belonged to ourselves. In other words, fallen humanity is not simply an imperfect creature in need of improvement; we are rebellious beings who must surrender and lay down our arms. Surrendering, apologizing, realizing that we've been on the wrong path, and being willing to start over from scratch—that's the only way out of the predicament. This process of surrender, this backward movement at full speed, is what Christians call repentance. However, repentance is far from enjoyable. It's much more challenging than merely swallowing our pride. It requires us to unlearn all the self-importance and self-will that we have cultivated for centuries. It involves killing a part of ourselves, experiencing a kind of death. Indeed, it takes a good person to truly repent. And here's the catch: Only a bad person needs to repent, but the worse we are, the more we need it, and the less we're able to do it. Can we repent with God's help? Yes, but what do we mean when we talk about God helping us? We mean that God imparts a piece of Himself to us, so to speak. He gives us a share of His reasoning abilities, allowing us to think. He instills a portion of His love in us, enabling us to love one another. When you teach a child to write, you guide their hand as they form the letters. They can form the letters because you are forming them. We love and reason because God loves and reasons, and He guides us in doing so. So, if we hadn't fallen, everything would be straightforward. Unfortunately, we now need God's assistance to do something that God Himself never does—surrender, suffer, submit, and die. There's nothing in God's nature that corresponds to this process. Thus, the road where we most need God's guidance is one God, by His very nature, has never traversed. God can only share what He possesses, and this particular aspect is absent from His nature.

However, let's imagine that God became a man. Suppose our human nature, which is susceptible to suffering and death, merged with God's nature in one person. In that case, this person could help us. They could surrender their will, suffer, and die because they are human. And they could do it perfectly because they are God. You and I can go through this process only if God does it within us. But God can only do it if He becomes human. That's why He pays our debt and endures what He Himself doesn't need to suffer at all.

I've heard people complain that if Jesus was both God and man, then His suffering and death lose their value because "it must have been so easy for Him." Others might rightly criticize the ingratitude and ungraciousness of this objection. What surprises me is the misunderstanding behind it. In a sense, those who make this objection are correct. They've even underestimated their own argument. The perfect submission, suffering, and death were easier for Jesus because He was God, but they were possible only because He was God. However, that's not a reason to reject them. The teacher can guide a child's hand in forming letters because the teacher is grown-up and knows how to write. The teacher finds it easier, and only because it's easier can they assist the child. If the child rejected the teacher because "it's easy for grown-ups" and instead waited to learn writing from another child who couldn't write (to avoid any "unfair" advantage), they wouldn't make much progress. If I'm drowning in a fast-flowing river, a person who still has one foot on the riverbank can extend their hand and save my life. Should I shout back (between gasps for air), "No, it's not fair! You have an advantage! You're keeping one foot on the bank"? That advantage, if you want to call it "unfair," is the only reason they can be of any assistance to me. Whom should we turn to for help if we don't turn to that which is stronger than ourselves?

That's how I perceive the Christian belief in the Atonement. However, remember that this is just one more illustration. Don't mistake it for the actual event. If it doesn't help you, feel free to disregard it.

The Practical Conclusion:

The ultimate surrender and humiliation were experienced by Christ. They were perfect because He was both God and man. The Christian belief states that if we somehow share in Christ's humility and suffering, we will also share in His victory over death and find a new life after our own deaths. In this new life, we will become perfect and perfectly happy beings. This goes beyond simply trying to follow His teachings. People often wonder when the next stage of evolution, a step beyond humanity, will occur. But from a Christian perspective, it has already happened. In Christ, a new kind of human emerged, and the new kind of life that began in Him is meant to be imparted to us. How is this accomplished? Let's recall how we acquired our ordinary, natural lives. We received them from our parents and ancestors without our consent, through a peculiar process involving pleasure, pain, and danger. It's a process that most of us spend years in childhood trying to understand, and some children initially find it hard to believe. It's indeed quite strange. The same God who devised this process of natural life is the one who determines how the new kind of life, the Christ life, is to be spread. We should be prepared for it to be equally peculiar. Just as He didn't consult us when He invented the process of reproduction, He doesn't consult us when it comes to this new life.

There are three things that serve as conduits for the Christ life to reach us: baptism, belief, and the mysterious action that different Christians refer to by various names—Holy

Communion, the Mass, or the Lord's Supper. These are the three common methods, although I'm not discounting the possibility of special cases where it is communicated without one or more of these. I don't have time to delve into those exceptional situations, and my knowledge on the subject is limited. When you're trying to explain to someone how to get to Edinburgh in a short amount of time, you would mention the trains. While it's true that one could also get there by boat or plane, you wouldn't necessarily bring up those options. Similarly, I won't discuss which of these three things is the most crucial. My Methodist friend would prefer me to emphasize belief and downplay the others, but I won't go into that. Anyone who claims to teach you Christian doctrine will tell you to utilize all three, and that's sufficient for our current purpose.

I personally don't understand why these things serve as conduits for the new life, but then again, I never saw any connection between a specific physical pleasure and the birth of a new human being. We must accept reality as it presents itself. There's no point in discussing how things should be or what we might have expected. Even though I can't comprehend why, I can explain why I believe it to be true. I have already explained why I have to believe that Jesus was and is God. It is also evident from historical records that He taught His followers that the new life is communicated in this manner. In other words, I believe it based on His authority. Don't be alarmed by the word "authority." Believing something on authority simply means believing it because you have been told by someone you consider trustworthy. Ninety-nine percent of the things we believe are believed on authority. I believe there is a place called New York, even though I haven't seen it myself. I cannot prove its existence through abstract reasoning. I believe it because reliable individuals have informed me about it. The average person believes in the Solar System, atoms, and blood circulation on authority because scientists assert them. Every historical statement in the world is believed on authority. None of us have witnessed the Norman Conquest or the defeat of the Spanish Armada. We couldn't prove them through pure logical deduction as one does in mathematics. We believe them because people who witnessed those events left written accounts, which we accept on authority. A person who rejects authority in matters of religion as some people do would have to resign themselves to knowing nothing throughout their life.

Please don't think that I am suggesting baptism, belief, and Holy Communion as substitutes for your own efforts to imitate Christ. Your natural life is inherited from your parents, but that doesn't mean it will stay that way if you do nothing about it. You can lose it through neglect, or you can extinguish it by committing suicide. You have to nurture and take care of it. But always remember that you are not creating it; you are simply maintaining a life that you received from someone else. Similarly, a Christian can lose the Christ life that has been given to them and must make efforts to preserve it. However, even the most virtuous Christian is not acting independently. They are nourishing and safeguarding a life they could never acquire through their own efforts alone. And this has practical implications. As long as the natural life is within your body, it contributes significantly to the healing and restoration of that body. If you get injured, your body can heal to some extent, unlike a dead body. A living body is not one that never experiences harm, but one that can repair itself to a certain degree. Likewise, a Christian is not someone who never makes mistakes but is someone who is enabled to repent, pick themselves up, and start over again after each stumble because the Christ life is within them, constantly restoring them. It allows them to participate, to some extent, in the voluntary death that Christ Himself underwent.

This sets the Christian apart from other individuals who strive to be good. They hope that by being good, they will please God if He exists, or at the very least, earn the approval of good people. However, Christians believe that any goodness they exhibit comes from the Christ life within them. They don't believe that God will love us because we are good, but rather that God will make us good because He loves us. It's similar to how a greenhouse roof doesn't attract the sun because it's bright, but rather it becomes bright because the sun shines upon it.

Let me clarify that when Christians speak of the Christ life being in them, they don't mean it in a purely mental or moral sense. They are not simply saying that they think about Christ or imitate Him. They mean that Christ is actively working through them. Collectively, all Christians form the physical body through which Christ operates. We are like His fingers, muscles, and cells. And perhaps this explains a couple of things. It clarifies why the new life is spread not only through purely mental acts like belief but also through physical acts like baptism and Holy Communion. It is not merely the spreading of an idea; it is more akin to biological or super-biological evolution. There's no point in trying to be more spiritual than God. God never intended for humans to be purely spiritual beings. That's why He utilizes physical elements like bread and wine to infuse the new life within us. We might consider this crude and unspiritual, but God doesn't. He invented eating. He delights in matter. He created it.

Another potential objection is the fairness of confining this new life to people who have heard of Christ and been able to believe in Him. However, God hasn't revealed His plans for those who are unaware of Him. We do know that no one can be saved except through Christ, but we don't know if only those who are aware of Him can be saved through Him. If you're concerned

about those outside of this knowledge, the m
thing you can do is to remain outside yo
constitute the body of Christ, the organism th
operates. Each additional person added to that
Him to do more. If you want to help those o
join and add your own unique contributior
Christ. Cutting off a man's fingers wouldn't be
to increase his productivity.

Another question that may arise is why God ch
this world, which is under enemy control, ir
establish a secret society to undermine the dev
He invade forcefully? Is it because He lacks
Christians believe that He will eventually inva
although we don't know when. However, we ca
why He delays. He desires to give us the oppor
choose His side. Imagine if a Frenchman waited
were already marching into Germany before an
allegiance to their cause. God will indeed launc
invasion. But I wonder if those who ask God to inte
and directly in our world truly comprehend what i
when He does. When that time comes, it will be th
world. It's like when the author steps onto the stage
the conclusion of the play. God will invade witho
and it will be an overwhelming event that ev
irresistible love or irresistible horror in every creatur
something so astonishingly beautiful to some and te
others that none of us will have any choice left. This
time for making a choice; it will be the moment
discover which side we had truly chosen, whether
aware of it or not. Now, at this very moment, we
opportunity to choose the right side. God is withho
final intervention to give us this chance. But it won't la
We must seize it or let it go.

BOOK III
CHRISTIAN BEHAVIOUR

THE THREE PARTS OF MORALITY

There's a story about a schoolboy who was asked what he thought God was like. His answer was that God seemed like someone who's always watching to see if anyone is having fun and then trying to stop it. Unfortunately, that's the kind of idea that many people have when they hear the word "morality." They see it as something that interferes and prevents them from enjoying themselves. But in reality, moral rules are like instructions for running the human machine. Each moral rule is there to prevent breakdowns, strains, or conflicts in the functioning of that machine. That's why these rules may initially feel like they're constantly going against our natural inclinations. When you're learning to use a machine, the instructor keeps telling you, "No, don't do it like that," because there are many things that may seem natural to you but don't actually work.

Some people prefer to talk about moral "ideals" rather than moral rules and "idealism" rather than moral obedience. It's true that moral perfection is an ideal in the sense that we can never fully achieve it. In that sense, all forms of perfection are ideals for us humans. We can't become perfect car drivers, perfect tennis players, or draw perfectly straight lines. But it's misleading to call moral perfection only an ideal. When someone says that a certain person, house, ship, or garden is "their ideal," they don't mean that everyone else should have the same ideal. We're allowed to have different tastes and different ideals in such matters. However, it's dangerous to describe someone who genuinely strives to keep the moral law as a person of "high ideals" because it might lead us to believe that moral perfection is merely their personal preference, and the rest of us are not obligated to pursue it. That would be a grave mistake. Perfect behavior may be unattainable, just like perfect gear-changing when we drive [with a manual transmission], but it's still a necessary ideal for all human beings, dictated by the nature of the human machine, just as perfect gear-changing is an ideal for all drivers, dictated by the nature of cars. It would be even more dangerous to consider oneself a person of "high ideals" simply because one tries to tell no lies at all (instead of only a few lies), or never commits adultery (instead of doing so only rarely) or refrains from being a bully (instead of being only moderately so). This mindset might lead to becoming self-righteous and thinking of oneself as a special person deserving congratulations for their "idealism." In reality, it would be akin to expecting applause for attempting to do a mathematic problem correctly at every step. Sure, perfect mathematics is an ideal, and we'll certainly make mistakes in calculations. But it would be foolish not to strive for accuracy since every mistake will cause trouble later. Similarly, every moral failure will lead to trouble, likely for others and definitely for oneself. By focusing on rules and obedience instead of "ideals" and "idealism," we remind ourselves of these realities.

Let's take another step forward. The human machine can malfunction in two ways. First, individuals can drift apart or collide with one another, causing harm through cheating or bullying. Second, things can go wrong within each individual, with different parts (faculties, desires, etc.) either drifting apart or interfering with one another. You can visualize this as a fleet of ships sailing in formation. The voyage will be successful if the ships don't collide or obstruct each other and if each ship is in good working order. In reality, you can't have one without the other. If the ships keep colliding, they won't remain seaworthy for long. Similarly, if their steering mechanisms are faulty, they won't be able to avoid collisions. Alternatively, think of humanity as a band playing a tune. To achieve a good result, two things are necessary: each player's individual instrument must be in tune, and they must all play at the right time to harmonize with one another.

However, there's one aspect we haven't considered yet. We haven't asked where the fleet is trying to go or what piece of music the band is trying to play. It matters greatly whether the fleet is aiming for New York but ends up in Calcutta, or if the band is hired to play dance music but only performs funeral marches.

While morality is concerned with three things; firstly, with fair play and harmony between individuals, secondly, involves tidying up and harmonizing the internal aspects within each individual. And thirdly, morality addresses the general purpose of human life as a whole, the reason for our existence, e.g., the course the entire fleet should take, and the tune the band conductor wants to hear.

You may have noticed that modern people often think primarily about the first aspect and overlook the other two. When people talk about striving for Christian moral standards, they usually mean promoting kindness and fairness among nations, classes, and individuals. They focus solely on the first aspect. When someone says that an action can't be wrong if it doesn't harm others, they're only considering the first aspect. They think it doesn't matter how their ship is on the inside, as long as they don't collide with other ships. It's natural to begin with this aspect of social relations since the negative consequences of poor morality in this sphere are evident and impact us every day. We witness war, poverty, corruption, lies, and shoddy work. Furthermore, almost everyone agrees (in theory) that human beings should be honest, kind, and helpful to one another. But if our thinking stops there, it's as if we haven't really thought at all. Unless we progress to the second aspect, which concerns morality within the individual, we're deceiving ourselves.

What's the use of giving instructions on how to steer ships to avoid collisions if the ships are so old and unreliable that they can't be steered at all? What's the point of creating rules for social behavior on paper if our own greed, cowardice, bad temper, and arrogance will prevent us from following them? I don't mean to say that we shouldn't think about improving our social and economic system. What I mean is that all that thinking will be meaningless unless we understand that only the courage and selflessness of individuals can truly make any system function properly. It's easy enough to eliminate specific forms of corruption or bullying that occur under the current system, but as long as people remain dishonest or abusive, they will find new ways to continue their harmful behavior under a different system. Laws cannot make people good, and without good individuals, we cannot have a good society. That's why we need to consider the second aspect: morality within each person.

However, we can't stop there either. We're now reaching a point where different beliefs about the universe lead to different behaviors. At first, it may seem reasonable to avoid discussing this and focus only on the moral principles that sensible people agree upon. But can we? Remember that religion involves statements about facts that are either true or false. If they are true, they lead to one set of conclusions about how to live a morally upright life. If they are false, the conclusions are entirely different. For example, consider someone who claims that an action isn't wrong unless it harms another person. They might understand that they shouldn't harm other ships in a convoy, but they believe that what they do to their own ship is their own business. But doesn't it make a significant difference whether they own the ship themselves or if they are merely occupants, accountable to the true owner? If someone else created them for their own purposes, then they have certain responsibilities that they wouldn't have if they simply belonged to themselves.

Moreover, Christianity asserts that every individual will live forever, and this claim is either true or false. If it's true, then many things that might not be worth considering if we only lived for seventy years become crucial matters if we're going to exist eternally. For example, our bad temper or jealousy might gradually worsen over time, seemingly insignificant within seventy years but potentially unbearable in a million years. In fact, if Christianity is true, Hell would be the accurate term for such unbearable conditions. Immortality also brings another distinction, which is connected to the difference between totalitarianism and democracy. If individuals live for only seventy years, then a state, nation, or civilization that lasts for a thousand years might appear more important than an individual life. However, if Christianity is true, then the individual becomes not only more important but immensely more significant, as their existence is everlasting, while the life of a state or civilization is only a fleeting moment.

Therefore, when contemplating morality, we must consider all three aspects: relations between people, the internal qualities of individuals, and the relationship between humans and the higher power that created them. We can all cooperate in the first aspect, but disagreements arise in the second and become more profound in the third. It's in addressing the third aspect that the main differences between Christian and non-Christian morality become apparent. For the rest of this book, I will assume the

Christian perspective and examine the entire picture as it would be if Christianity is true.

In the next section, I want to introduce another way in which the subject of morality has been divided by ancient writers. The longer scheme involves seven virtues, with four of them known as the "Cardinal" virtues and the remaining three as the "Theological" virtues. The Cardinal virtues are those recognized by all civilized people, while the Theological virtues are typically known only by Christians. In this discussion, I will focus on the four Cardinal virtues: Prudence, Temperance, Justice, and Fortitude.

Prudence[17] refers to practical common sense, taking the time to think about one's actions and the potential consequences. Nowadays, people often overlook Prudence as a virtue. Some Christians mistakenly believe that being "good" means it doesn't matter if they lack wisdom. However, Jesus' statement about being childlike refers to innocence, not intellectual immaturity. In fact, Jesus told us to be both innocent and wise. He wants us to have the simplicity, affection, and teachability of a child, but also to engage our intelligence fully and be mentally prepared. While God accommodates individuals with limited intellect, He expects everyone to utilize the intelligence they have. The motto shouldn't be "Be good and let others be clever," but rather "Be good and recognize that it involves being as intelligent as possible." God doesn't favor intellectual laziness any more than any other form of laziness. If you're considering becoming a Christian, be aware that it requires your full commitment, including the use of your intellect. Fortunately, it works the other way around as well. When someone genuinely strives to be a Christian, their intelligence will sharpen.

---

[17] Prudence: the ability to govern and discipline oneself by the use of reason.

Christianity itself is an educational path, which is why uneducated believers like Bunyan can produce astounding works[18].

Temperance[19] is a term that has changed in meaning. Nowadays, it's often associated with abstaining from alcohol entirely. However, when the second Cardinal virtue was named "Temperance," it had a different connotation. Temperance wasn't solely about abstaining but rather about finding the right balance in all pleasures. It's a mistake to think that all Christians should be teetotalers. Islam, not Christianity, advocates complete abstinence from alcohol. Of course, certain Christians may choose to abstain from alcohol for specific reasons — perhaps they cannot handle it responsibly, want to allocate the money to the poor, or avoid encouraging others prone to drunkenness. The key point is that they are abstaining from something they do not condemn and are happy to see others enjoy. One indication of a certain kind of bad person is their inability to give up something without demanding that everyone else does the same. That's not the Christian way. While an individual Christian might decide to give up various things for personal reasons, such as marriage, meat, beer, or movies, the moment they start condemning those things or looking down on others who indulge in them, they have taken the wrong path.

A great harm has been done by limiting the term "Temperance" to the question of alcohol. This narrow definition causes people to forget that intemperance applies to many other things. A person who obsesses over golf or their motorcycle, or a woman who dedicates all her thoughts to clothes, bridge, or her dog, is just as intemperate as someone who gets drunk every evening.

---

[18] John Bunyan authored *The Pilgrim's Progress* while in jail.
[19] Temperance: moderation in action, thought, or feeling.

While addiction to bridge or golf may not manifest in stumbling on the street, God isn't fooled by external appearances.

Justice[20] encompasses more than what takes place in law courts. It represents fairness, honesty, integrity, keeping promises, and all aspects of righteous living. Fortitude[21], on the other hand, encompasses both physical and moral courage—the ability to face danger and endure pain. It can be summed up as having "guts." Interestingly, you'll notice that practicing any of the other virtues for an extended period requires fortitude.

One more point about virtues deserves attention. There is a distinction between performing a specific just or temperate action and embodying justice or temperance as a person. Someone who isn't a skilled tennis player may occasionally make a good shot. But what defines a good player is the reliability of their eye, muscles, and nerves, developed through countless good shots. Even when they're not playing, there's a certain quality or character present, just as a mathematician's mind possesses a particular habit and outlook beyond mathematical calculations. Similarly, a person who consistently acts justly develops a particular quality of character. It's this quality that truly matters when we speak of "virtue." This distinction is important because if we only focus on the specific actions, three misconceptions can arise.

(1)   We might believe that as long as we do the right thing, it doesn't matter how or why we do it—whether willingly or unwillingly, cheerfully or reluctantly, driven by public opinion or personal conviction. However, the truth is that performing

---

[20] Justice: the maintenance or administration of what is just especially by the impartial adjustment of conflicting claims or the assignment of merited rewards or punishments.

[21] Fortitude: strength of mind that enables a person to encounter danger or bear pain or adversity with courage.

the right actions for the wrong reasons doesn't contribute to the development of the internal virtue or character that truly matters. If a bad tennis player hits a powerful shot not because they recognize the need for a powerful stroke, but out of frustration, that shot might help them win a particular game by chance. However, it won't contribute to their growth as a reliable player.

(2)   We might think that God only desires obedience to a set of rules, whereas He actually seeks individuals of a specific kind.

(3)   We might assume that virtues are only necessary in this present life, that in the afterlife, where there is no conflict, there would be no need for justice or courage. While it's true that there may be no occasion for just or courageous acts in the next world, there will always be a need to possess the qualities that can only be developed through such acts in this world. The point is not that God will reject someone from eternal life if they lack certain character qualities, but rather that without at least the beginnings of those qualities, no external conditions could create true happiness—an unshakeable, profound happiness that God intends for us.

SOCIAL MORALITY

When it comes to morality between people, it's important to understand that Christ didn't come to preach a completely new morality. The Golden Rule of the New Testament (Do as you would be done by) simply summarizes what everyone has always known to be right. True moral teachers don't introduce new moralities; it's usually misguided individuals who do that. As Dr. Samuel L. Johnson said, "People need reminders more than they need instruction." The real task of a moral teacher is to repeatedly bring us back to the old, simple principles that we often overlook, like guiding a horse back to a fence it refuses to jump or helping a child grasp a lesson they want to avoid.

It's also essential to recognize that Christianity doesn't provide a detailed political plan for applying the Golden Rule to a specific society at a specific time. It couldn't, because its message is meant for all people at all times, and what works in one place or era might not work in another. Moreover, Christianity doesn't aim to replace or supersede other areas of human knowledge and expertise. Instead, it serves as a guide, directing those areas toward the right path and infusing them with new life if they're willing to align with its principles.

When people say, "The Church should lead us," they should mean the entire body of practicing Christians. The Church should set an example through individuals who possess the right talents, such as economists and statesmen. All economists and statesmen should be Christians, and their efforts in politics and economics should be focused on putting the Golden Rule into action. If this were to happen, and if the rest of us were genuinely receptive, we would find Christian solutions to our social problems more quickly. Unfortunately, when people ask for leadership from the Church, they often expect the clergy to present a specific political agenda. That's not realistic. The clergy are a specific group within the Church who have been specially trained to attend to our eternal concerns. We're asking them to perform a different role for which they haven't been trained. The responsibility falls on us, the laypeople. The application of Christian principles, in areas like trade unionism or education, should come from Christian trade unionists, Christian schoolmasters, Christian novelists, and Christian dramatists — not from the bishops attempting to write plays and novels in their spare time.

However, even without going into specifics, the New Testament gives us a glimpse of what a fully Christian society would be like. It might provide more than we can fully embrace. It emphasizes that there should be no freeloaders or parasites — those who don't work shouldn't eat. Everyone should engage in productive work that yields something beneficial. There shouldn't be the production of unnecessary luxury goods or misleading advertisements to convince us to buy them. Arrogance and pretentiousness should be absent. In this sense, a Christian society might align with what we now call leftist ideals. On the other hand, Christianity also emphasizes obedience — obedience and outward respect for properly appointed authorities, from children to parents, and, though unpopular, from wives to husbands. Thirdly, a Christian society should be characterized by cheerfulness, filled with singing and rejoicing, while regarding worry or anxiety as wrong. Courtesy is valued, and the New Testament discourages what it calls "busybodies."

If such a society existed and we visited it, we might have a mixed impression. Its economic life might be very socialistic and "advanced," but its family life and code of manners might be rather old-fashioned, even ceremonious and aristocratic. Each of us might appreciate certain aspects of it, but very few would embrace the entire society. This is expected because we have all deviated from the total plan of Christianity in different ways, and each person wants to present their own modifications as the actual plan. This is why progress is limited, and it allows people with opposing views to claim they are fighting for Christianity.

Now, let's consider another point. Ancient Greek, Jewish, and Christian teachings have advised against lending money at interest (usury). However, our modern economic system is built on this practice. Some argue that these teachings didn't anticipate joint-stock companies and only aimed to discourage private moneylenders, so we shouldn't be concerned about what they said. I can't provide a definitive answer on this matter since I'm not an economist. However, it's worth noting that three significant civilizations condemned the very practice on which our entire system is based.

One more point to discuss is charity-giving to the poor. It's an essential aspect of Christian morality, and it appears to be a pivotal point in the parable of the sheep and the goats. Some people today argue that charity should be unnecessary, and instead, we should focus on creating a society where there are no poor individuals to help. They may be right in striving for such a society, but if anyone thinks that, as a result, we can stop giving to those in need, they have departed from Christian morality entirely. Determining how much we should give is challenging. It's safe to say that we should give more than we can comfortably spare. If our spending on comforts, luxuries, and entertainment aligns with what others with similar income levels consider standard, we're probably giving too little. If our charitable contributions don't pinch or inconvenience us, they're likely too small. Our charitable giving should sometimes prevent us from doing things we'd like to do but can't because of our financial commitment to helping others. This primarily applies to general acts of charity. Specific cases of distress among our relatives, friends, neighbors, or employees, which God seems to bring to our attention, may demand much more from us, even if it risks our own position. For many of us, the main obstacle to charity isn't luxurious living or the desire for more money but rather the fear of insecurity. This temptation must be recognized. Additionally, our pride can hinder our charity. We may be tempted to spend more than necessary on showy displays of generosity, such as tipping and hospitality, while neglecting those who genuinely require our assistance.

Before I conclude, I want to make a guess about how this section may have affected readers. I suspect that some Leftist individuals may be upset because they feel it hasn't gone far enough in their direction, while individuals with opposing views may be angry because they believe it has gone too far. This highlights the challenge in developing blueprints for a Christian society. Most of us aren't genuinely seeking to understand what Christianity teaches; instead, we approach it with the hope of finding support for our own political views. We're searching for an ally when we're offered either a Master or a Judge. I'm no exception—I too wanted to omit certain parts of this section. That's why such discussions will be futile unless we take a much longer route. A Christian society won't materialize until most of us genuinely desire it, and we won't desire it until we become fully Christian. I can repeat "Do as you would be done by" endlessly, but I can't truly live it out until I love my neighbor as myself. And I can't learn to love my neighbor as myself until I learn to love God. And the only way to learn to love God is by learning to obey Him. Thus, as I warned earlier, our focus shifts from social matters to religious matters. The longest way around turns out to be the shortest way home.

MORALITY AND PSYCHOANALYSIS

I've mentioned that in order to have a Christian society, most of us need to become Christian individuals. However, this doesn't mean we should delay taking action in society until some distant future. It means we should begin both tasks simultaneously: (1) figuring out how to apply "Do as you would be done by" to modern society, and (2) striving to become the kind of people who would genuinely apply it if we understood how.

Before delving into specifics, there are two general points I'd like to address. Firstly, I want to discuss the relationship between Christian morality and psychoanalysis[22], a technique that claims to address similar issues. It's important to differentiate between the actual medical theories and techniques employed by psychoanalysts and the broader philosophical views added by figures like Freud. Freud's philosophy contradicts Christianity and is also at odds with the views of another renowned psychologist, Jung. While Freud's psychoanalysis may be valuable in treating neuroses, his philosophical ideas are not in line with Christian principles. Nonetheless, psychoanalysis itself, apart from Freud's

---

[22] Psychoanalysis: a system of psychological theory and therapy that aims to treat mental conditions by investigating the interaction of conscious and unconscious elements in the mind and bringing repressed fears and conflicts into the conscious mind by techniques such as dream interpretation and free association.

additions, is not inherently contradictory to Christianity. It can overlap with Christian morality in certain areas, and it wouldn't hurt for clergy members to have some knowledge of it. However, the two techniques serve different purposes.

When a person makes a moral choice, two factors come into play. One is the act of choosing itself, and the other is the various emotions, impulses, and other psychological aspects that influence the decision. This psychological aspect can be categorized as either normal, consisting of feelings common to all humans, or abnormal, arising from subconscious issues. For example, a rational fear of danger would be a normal feeling, whereas an irrational fear of cats or spiders would be an abnormal one. Similarly, a natural desire for a person of the opposite sex is normal, while a perverted[23] desire for someone of the same sex is abnormal. Psychoanalysis aims to address these abnormal feelings and provide individuals with improved psychological material for making choices. On the other hand, morality focuses on the acts of choice themselves.

To illustrate this, let's imagine three men going to war. The first man experiences the normal fear of danger but overcomes it through moral effort, becoming brave. The other two men, due to issues in their subconscious, have exaggerated and irrational fears that cannot be resolved through moral effort alone. Now, suppose a psychoanalyst successfully treats these two men, restoring them to the same position as the first man. At this point, the psychoanalytical problem is solved, and the moral problem emerges. Even though they are now cured and possess similar psychological material, these two men may choose different paths. The first man might say, "Thank goodness I've overcome those irrational fears. Now I can fulfill my duty to the

---

[23] Pervert: to cause to turn aside or away from what is good or true or morally.

cause of freedom as I've always wanted." However, the second man might say, "Well, I'm glad I no longer feel as frightened, but that doesn't change the fact that I'm still determined to prioritize myself and let others take on the dangerous tasks. In fact, feeling less afraid allows me to protect myself more effectively and hide it from others." This difference is purely moral, and psychoanalysis cannot address it. Regardless of how much their psychological material improves, their free choice on how to prioritize themselves remains, which is the core concern of morality.

The unhealthy psychological manifestation is not a sin but a disease that requires healing, not repentance. This is crucial to understand. Human beings judge each other based on external actions, but God judges us based on our moral choices. When a person with a pathological fear of cats forces themselves to pick one up for a good reason, they may display more courage in God's eyes than a healthy individual who receives a Victoria Cross for bravery. Similarly, when someone who has been perverted from youth and taught that cruelty is acceptable performs a small act of kindness or refrains from cruelty, even risking ridicule from their peers, they may, in God's eyes, surpass the benevolence of someone willing to sacrifice their life for a friend.

It's worth examining this from another angle. Some seemingly nice individuals may have made such poor use of their favorable upbringing and circumstances that they are worse than individuals considered fiendish. Can we be certain about how we would behave if burdened with their psychological makeup, combined with a troubled upbringing and the power, for instance, of Heinrich Himmler? That's why Christians are advised not to judge others.

We can only observe the outcomes of a person's choices based on their psychological makeup. However, God doesn't judge them solely on their raw material but on what they have done with it. Most of a person's psychological makeup is likely influenced by their body, and when their body dies, those influences will fall away, leaving the core self—the one that makes choices—exposed. All the things we attributed to ourselves, like good digestion leading to positive traits, will be discarded for some of us. Likewise, negative traits resulting from complexes or poor health will no longer define others. For the first time, we will see everyone as they truly were, leading to surprises.

This brings me to my second point. People often view Christian morality as a transaction, where God says, "If you follow a set of rules, I will reward you, and if you don't, I will punish you." However, I believe there's a better way to understand it. Each time you make a choice, you are shaping the core part of yourself—the part that chooses—into something slightly different than before. Throughout your life, with countless choices, you are gradually transforming this core into either a heavenly or hellish creature. Becoming a heavenly creature means attaining joy, peace, knowledge, and power while being in harmony with God, other creatures, and oneself. Becoming a hellish creature results in madness, horror, idiocy, rage, impotence, and eternal loneliness. Every one of us, at every moment, is progressing towards one of these states.

This explains a puzzling aspect of Christian writers. They may seem incredibly strict about minor thoughts, yet surprisingly forgiving about heinous acts of murder and betrayal, emphasizing the possibility of forgiveness through repentance. I've come to realize they are right. They are always considering the impact an action has on the hidden core self, which remains unseen in this life but will be experienced for eternity. A person in a position where their anger leads to the deaths of thousands may, in God's eyes, demonstrate more courage than a healthy person who receives a prestigious military honor. Each person, if genuinely turning to God, can have their distorted core self-corrected. Ultimately, whether an action is significant or trivial from an external perspective is not what truly matters.

Lastly, remember that the right path not only leads to peace but also to knowledge. As a person improves, they become more aware of the remaining evil within them. Conversely, as a person worsens, they become less aware of their own wrongdoing. A moderately bad person recognizes their shortcomings, while a thoroughly bad person believes they are perfectly fine. This is simply common sense. You understand sleep when you are awake, not when you're asleep. Mistakes in mathematics become clear when your mind is functioning properly, not when you're making them. You comprehend the nature of drunkenness when you're sober, not when you're drunk. Good people understand both good and evil, while bad people understand neither.

SEXUAL MORALITY

Now let's talk about Christian views on sex, specifically the virtue of chastity. It's important not to confuse Christian chastity with societal notions of "modesty" in the sense of propriety and decency. Social standards of propriety dictate how much of the human body should be shown and what topics can be discussed using which words, based on the customs of a particular social group. While the rule of chastity remains the same for all Christians throughout history, the rule of propriety changes over time. For example, a girl in the Pacific islands wearing minimal clothing and a Victorian lady fully covered in garments could both be considered equally modest and proper within their respective societies, even though we can't determine their level of chastity based on their clothing alone. In Shakespeare's time, chaste women may have used language that would be considered extremely inappropriate in the nineteenth century. Breaking the rule of propriety in order to incite lust in oneself or others is considered offensive to chastity. However, breaking it out of ignorance or carelessness is merely a matter of bad manners. When people deliberately break the rule to shock or embarrass others, they may not necessarily be unchaste, but they are being unkind, as it is uncharitable to take pleasure in making others uncomfortable. I don't believe that strict adherence to propriety is proof of chastity or helps promote it. Therefore, I consider the relaxation and simplification of these rules that has occurred in my lifetime to be a positive development. However, the current challenge is that people of different ages and backgrounds don't all agree on the same standards, and this creates confusion. During this period of confusion, I believe older or traditional individuals should be cautious about assuming that younger or "liberated" individuals are corrupt simply because they don't adhere to the old standards. Similarly, young people should not label their elders as prudish or puritanical just because they are hesitant to adopt the new standards. Most problems can be resolved by genuinely wanting to believe the best about others and making them as comfortable as possible.

Chastity is often considered the least popular of the Christian virtues. There's no denying it: according to the old Christian rule, you can either be married and completely faithful to your partner, or you can choose complete abstinence. This is so difficult and goes against our natural instincts that it raises a question: either Christianity is mistaken, or our sexual instincts, as they are now, have gone awry. It must be one or the other. As a Christian, I believe it is our instincts that have gone awry, but I have other reasons for thinking so.

The biological purpose of sex is procreation, just as the biological purpose of eating is nourishing the body. If we eat whenever we feel like it and as much as we want, most of us will certainly overeat, but not to an extreme degree. One person may eat enough for two, but not enough for ten. Our appetite slightly exceeds its biological purpose, but not to a significant extent. On the other hand, if a healthy young man indulged in sexual activity whenever he felt inclined and each act resulted in a child, within ten years he could easily populate a small village. This demonstrates an absurd and excessive appetite that surpasses its function.

Let's consider another example. A striptease act can attract a large audience, with people watching a person undress on stage. Now, imagine a country where a theatre could be filled simply by bringing a covered plate on stage and slowly revealing, just before the lights go out, that it contains a lamb chop or a piece of bacon. In such a country, wouldn't you think something had gone wrong with their appetite for food? Similarly, anyone from a different world would find something equally peculiar about the state of the sex instinct among us.

One critic suggested that if he found a country where striptease acts with food were popular, he would conclude that the people in that country were starving. By this, he meant that such striptease acts were not a result of sexual corruption but rather a consequence of sexual deprivation. I agree with him that if we discovered similar acts involving food in a strange land, one possible explanation would be famine. However, the next step would be to investigate whether people in that country were actually consuming more or less food. If the evidence showed that they were eating plentifully, then we would have to discard the hypothesis of starvation and search for another explanation. Likewise, before accepting sexual deprivation as the cause of striptease acts, we should examine whether our age exhibits more sexual abstinence than past eras when such acts were unknown. However, there is no evidence to support the notion of widespread sexual deprivation today. Contraception has made sexual indulgence easier and safer, both within and outside of marriage, than ever before. Public opinion is also more accepting of illicit relationships and even perversions than it has been since ancient times. Additionally, the hypothesis of "starvation" is not the only one we can consider. It is well-known that our sexual appetite, like other appetites, grows stronger with indulgence. Starving individuals may think incessantly about food, but so do gluttons. Both the famished and the sated find pleasure in titillating experiences.

Here's another point to consider. Very few people have a desire to consume things that are not food or engage in activities with food other than eating it. In other words, perversions of the appetite for food are rare. However, perversions of the sex instinct are numerous, difficult to overcome, and horrifying. I apologize for delving into these details, but it is necessary. Over the past twenty years, you and I have been bombarded with continuous lies about sex. We've been incessantly told that sexual desire is just like any other natural desire, and if we abandon the outdated Victorian idea of suppressing it, everything will be fine. But it's not true. As soon as we examine the facts, beyond the propaganda, it becomes clear that it's not true.

They claim that sex has become problematic because it was suppressed. However, for the past two decades, it has not been suppressed; it has been openly discussed all the time. Yet, it remains a problem. If suppression were the cause of the issue, simply discussing it openly would have solved it. But it hasn't. I believe it's the other way around. I believe that human beings initially suppressed it because it had become such a mess. Modern individuals often say, "There's nothing to be ashamed of when it comes to sex." They might mean two things. First, they may imply that there is nothing to be ashamed of in the fact that the human race reproduces itself in a particular manner or that it derives pleasure from it. If that's what they mean, they are correct. Christianity also acknowledges this. It is not sex itself or the pleasure derived from it that is problematic. The old Christian teachers argued that if humanity had never fallen, sexual pleasure would be even greater than it is now. Some confused Christians have wrongly suggested that Christianity views sex, the body, or pleasure itself as inherently bad. But they were mistaken. Christianity is one of the few major religions that wholeheartedly approves of the body, believing that matter is good. It recognizes that God Himself once took on a human body and that a form of bodily existence will be an integral part of our happiness, beauty, and vitality even in

Heaven. Christianity has celebrated marriage more than any other religion, and numerous love poems produced throughout history were written by Christians. So, if anyone claims that sex itself is bad, Christianity firmly contradicts them. However, when people say, "Sex is nothing to be ashamed of," they may be referring to the present state of the sexual instinct, which I believe is indeed something to be ashamed of.

If that's the case, I think they are mistaken. I believe it is something to be deeply ashamed of. There is nothing to be ashamed of in enjoying food. However, there would be plenty to be ashamed of if half the world made food the primary focus of their lives, spending their time looking at pictures of food and salivating over them. I am not implying that you and I are personally responsible for the current situation. Our ancestors passed down to us predispositions that are warped in this area, and we grow up surrounded by propaganda that promotes unchastity. Some people want to keep our sexual instinct constantly inflamed in order to profit from it because an individual consumed by obsession has little resistance to sales tactics. God understands our circumstances, and He will not judge us as if we had no difficulties to overcome. What matters is the sincerity and perseverance of our will to overcome these challenges.

Before we can be healed, we must genuinely desire to be healed. Those who truly seek help will find it. Even when it seems that no help is forthcoming or we receive less help than we need, we should not lose hope. After every failure, we should ask for forgiveness, pick ourselves up, and try again. Often, what God initially helps us with is not the virtue itself, but rather the ability to keep trying. Even attempted virtue brings enlightenment, while indulgence leads to confusion.

Lastly, although I have discussed sex at length, I want to emphasize that it is not the central focus of Christian morality.

If anyone believes that Christians consider unchastity the greatest vice, they are mistaken. While sexual sins are certainly bad, they are the least severe of all sins. The most dreadful pleasures are purely spiritual: the pleasure derived from putting others in the wrong, from bossing people around, patronizing them, and engaging in gossip or backstabbing; the pleasures of power and hatred. Within me, there are two competing forces alongside my human self, which I strive to become. These forces are the Animal self and the Diabolical self. The Diabolical self is the more wicked of the two. That's why a cold, self-righteous individual who regularly attends church may be closer to hell than a prostitute. However, it is best to be neither.

CHRISTIAN MARRIAGE

In the previous chapter, I mostly talked about the issues with human sexual desires, but didn't focus much on how these desires could be properly managed, or in other words, through a Christian marriage. I haven't talked much about marriage for two reasons: firstly, Christian teachings on marriage aren't generally well-liked; and secondly, I've never been married, so I can only discuss it based on what I've learned from others. However, considering the topic's importance in Christian morals, I feel obliged to touch upon it.

According to Christianity, marriage is a bond where a man and woman become one entity, akin to a key and its lock, or a violin and its bow — they function best together. Any sexual relations outside of this marriage union is considered wrong, as it tries to separate the sexual aspect from the emotional, spiritual, and other bonds that form the complete union of marriage. Christianity doesn't reject sexual pleasure; it rejects separating this pleasure from the rest of the marital relationship.

Furthermore, Christianity promotes the idea that a marriage should last a lifetime. Different Christian denominations may have varying views on divorce, but they all agree divorce it is a major event — comparable to a physical amputation rather than just a simple relationship readjustment.

Marriage is also a matter of keeping a promise, which falls under the virtue of justice. Anyone married in a church has publicly promised to stick to their partner till death. Breaking this promise, like any other, is seen as dishonest.

The modern notion that "being in love" is the sole reason to stay married overlooks the promise and contract that marriage involves. This perspective diminishes the importance of love as a long-lasting commitment rather than a transient feeling. Christianity encourages lovers to take their commitments seriously, understanding that love evolves from passionate romance to a deeper unity sustained by deliberate effort and habit.

Many people erroneously believe that "being in love" should last forever, which is unrealistic and not necessarily desirable. Maintaining the thrill of early love can distract from developing deeper, more sustainable interest and love over time. Rather than chasing after old thrills, it's more fulfilling to embrace the evolution of experiences, which can lead to discovering new joys and passions in life.

Before dismissing my views due to my lack of personal marriage experience, consider if your judgments are based on real-life experiences or romanticized notions from novels and films. Remember that the thrill of new experiences, like being in love, learning to fly, or moving to a beautiful place, naturally fades over time, but this doesn't mean the experiences are not worth having. On the contrary, when you accept this natural course of events, you allow yourself to find new thrills and deeper happiness in life.

In novels and plays, we often get the idea that "falling in love" is an uncontrollable force, something that happens to us like catching an illness. Because of this belief, some married people give up when they feel attracted to someone new. However, I believe that these overwhelming passions are much less common in real life than in books, especially when we are mature. When we meet someone who is attractive, intelligent, and kind, it's natural to appreciate and love those qualities. But whether this love turns into what we call "being in love" is largely within our own control. If our minds are filled with romantic stories and songs, and if we consume alcohol excessively, we might transform any love we feel into that intense kind of love. It's similar to how rainwater naturally flows into a rut on a path or how wearing blue-tinted glasses makes everything appear blue. But we have the power to avoid this outcome by making conscious choices.

Now, let's discuss divorce, but let's separate two concepts that are often conflated. One is the Christian idea of marriage, and the other is whether Christians, as voters or Members of Parliament, should impose their views on marriage through divorce laws. Many people think that if you're a Christian, you should make divorce difficult for everyone. However, I don't agree with that perspective. Personally, I would be upset if Muslims tried to prevent us from drinking wine. I believe that the Church should acknowledge that the majority of British people are not Christians and, therefore, cannot be expected to live according to Christian principles. There should be two distinct types of marriage: one recognized by the State with rules that apply to all citizens, and another governed by the Church with its own rules for its members. This distinction should be clear so that people can differentiate between marriages in a Christian sense and those that are not.

Now, let's address the Christian notion of a wife obeying her husband and the idea that the man is the "head" of the household. Two questions naturally arise: First, why should there be a head at all? Why not equality? Second, if there must be a head, why does it have to be the man?

The need for a head arises from the belief in the permanence of marriage. As long as the husband and wife agree, the question of a head is irrelevant. We hope that agreement will be the norm in a Christian marriage. However, when a genuine disagreement arises, what should happen? Of course, they should discuss it, but let's assume they have already done so and failed to reach an agreement. What happens next? They cannot decide by majority vote because there are only two of them. In such a case, only two possibilities exist: they either separate and go their separate ways or one of them must have the final say. If marriage is meant to be permanent, one of them must ultimately have the power to make decisions regarding the family. A permanent association requires a structure.

Now, if there must be a head, why is it typically the man? Firstly, is there a genuine desire for it to be the woman? From what I observe, even women who want to be the head of their households often criticize and pity men who are dominated by their wives. They might say, "Poor Mr. X! I can't understand why he allows that bossy woman to control him." I don't think women feel particularly flattered when someone mentions their own "headship." There seems to be something unnatural about wives ruling over their husbands, as the wives themselves are somewhat ashamed of it and look down on the husbands they dominate. But there's another reason, and I'll be frank as a bachelor because this reason is easier to see from an outsider's perspective. When it comes to the family's relationship with the outside world, what we could call its foreign policy, it ultimately depends on the man because he should be, and usually is, more impartial towards outsiders. A woman primarily fights for her own children and husband against the rest of the world. Naturally, her claims and concerns take precedence over others. She is the primary guardian of their interests. The husband's role is to ensure that her natural bias doesn't become excessive. He has the final say to protect others from the intense loyalty the wife feels towards her family. If anyone doubts this, let me ask a simple question: If your dog bit the child next door or if your child hurt the dog next door, whom would you rather deal with, the master of the house or the mistress? Or, if you're a married woman, let me ask you this question. Even though you admire your husband, would you say that his main flaw is that he doesn't assert himself enough when it comes to standing up for his rights and yours against the neighbors? Does he tend to avoid confrontation, like someone who tries to keep the peace even if it means giving in too easily?

FORGIVENESS

Forgiveness is a topic that often receives mixed reactions. In a previous chapter, I mentioned that chastity is an unpopular virtue among Christians, but I now believe that the one I'm going to discuss today is even more unpopular: the Christian rule of "loving your neighbor as yourself." In Christian morality, "your neighbor" includes "your enemy," and this brings us face to face with the difficult duty of forgiving those who have wronged us. Everyone agrees that forgiveness is a beautiful idea until they have something to forgive, like during times of war. Bringing up the subject of forgiveness in such situations usually leads to anger and outrage. It's not that people think it's too challenging to practice this virtue; rather, they find it repulsive and contemptible. They claim that discussing forgiveness makes them sick. Some of you might even be thinking, "I wonder how you would feel about forgiving the Gestapo if you were a Pole or a Jew?"

And you know what? I wonder about that too. Just as when Christianity tells me that I shouldn't renounce my faith even if it means facing torture and death, I also wonder what I would do when confronted with that choice. In this book, I'm not trying to tell you what I would do because, honestly, I can do very little. I'm here to tell you what Christianity is. I didn't invent it. And right at the core of Christianity, I find the phrase, "Forgive us our sins as we forgive those who sin against us." There's not the slightest suggestion that we are offered forgiveness on any other terms. It's crystal clear that if we don't forgive, we won't be forgiven. There's no room for ambiguity. So, what should we do?

Forgiveness is going to be challenging no matter what, but I think there are two things we can do to make it easier. Just as in mathematics, you start with simple addition rather than jumping straight into calculus, if we genuinely want (and it all depends on truly wanting) to learn how to forgive, perhaps we should start with something easier than forgiving the Gestapo. We can start by forgiving our spouse, parents, children, or someone close to us for something they did or said in the past week. That will likely keep us occupied for now. Secondly, we can try to understand what it means to love our neighbor as ourselves. I am obligated to love my neighbor just as I love myself. But how exactly do I love myself?

Now that I think about it, I don't necessarily feel fondness or affection towards myself, and I don't always enjoy my own company. So, it seems that "loving your neighbor" doesn't mean "having warm feelings towards them" or "finding them attractive." I should have realized this earlier because, in reality, you can't force yourself to feel fond of someone. Do I think highly of myself? Do I consider myself a great person? Well, unfortunately, I sometimes do (and those are probably my worst moments), but that's not why I love myself. In fact, it's the other way around: my self-love leads me to think well of myself. But thinking well of myself isn't the reason why I love myself. So, apparently, loving my enemies doesn't mean thinking they're nice either. And that's a tremendous relief. Many people mistakenly believe that forgiving your enemies means pretending they are not as bad as they truly are, when it's quite evident that they are "that bad". Let's go a step further. In moments of clarity, I not only don't consider myself a good person, but I recognize that I have done some terrible things. I can't help but feel horrified and disgusted by some of my actions. So, apparently, I'm allowed to detest and hate the actions of my enemies. Now that I think about it, I recall Christian teachers telling me long ago that I should hate a bad person's actions but not hate the person themselves. They would say, "Hate the sin but not the sinner."

For a long time, I thought this was a silly, hair-splitting distinction. How could I hate what a person does without hating the person? However, years later, I realized that I had been doing this all my life with one person—myself. Despite disliking my own cowardice, conceit, or greed, I continued to love myself. There was never any difficulty with that. In fact, the reason I hated those things was precisely because I loved myself. It's because I loved myself that I felt sorry for being the type of person who engaged in such behavior. Consequently, Christianity doesn't want us to diminish in the slightest our hatred for cruelty and betrayal. We should hate those actions. Nothing we have said about them needs to be unsaid. However, Christianity does want us to hate them in the same way we hate our own flaws: being sorry that the person committed those actions and hoping, if possible, that somehow, someday, somewhere, they can be healed and restored as human beings.

Now, here's the real test. Imagine reading a news story about heinous atrocities. Then suppose something comes up suggesting that the story may not be entirely true or not as awful as it was initially reported. What is your first reaction? Is it, "Thank God, they aren't as bad as I thought," or is it a sense of disappointment and a determination to cling to the original story because it brings you pleasure to think of your enemies as utterly wicked? If your reaction is the latter, I'm afraid it's the first step in a process that, if taken to the extreme, will turn us into devils. You see, you're starting to wish that the blackness you perceive is even darker. If we allow that wish to flourish, eventually we'll want to see gray as black, and then even white itself as black. In the end, we'll insist on seeing everything — God, our friends, and even ourselves — as bad, and we won't be able to stop doing it. We'll be trapped forever in a realm of pure hatred.

Let's take it a step further. Does loving your enemy mean refraining from punishing them? No, because loving myself doesn't mean I shouldn't subject myself to punishment, even to the point of death. If I had committed murder, the right Christian thing to do would be to turn myself in to the authorities and face the consequences, even if it means being executed. Therefore, in my opinion, it's entirely justifiable for a Christian judge to sentence someone to death or for a Christian soldier to kill an enemy. I've always believed this since I became a Christian, even before the war, and I still believe it now that we are at peace. It's futile to quote "Thou shalt not kill." There are two Greek words: one for general killing and the other specifically for murder. When Christ quotes that commandment, He uses the word for murder in all three accounts — Matthew, Mark, and Luke. I'm told the same distinction exists in Hebrew. All killing is not murder, just as all sexual intercourse is not adultery. When soldiers approached John the Baptist asking what they should do, he never suggested that they should leave the army. Similarly, when Christ encountered a Roman centurion — a high-ranking soldier — he didn't tell him to abandon his profession. The idea of a knight, a Christian who fights in defense of a just cause, is one of the great concepts within Christianity. War is a terrible thing, and I can respect an honest pacifist, even though I believe they are entirely mistaken. What I can't comprehend is the kind of semi-pacifism prevalent today, which implies that although we have to fight, we should do it with a long face and a sense of shame. This attitude robs many courageous young Christians in the military of something they rightfully deserve—a natural accompanying spirit of joy and wholeheartedness.

I've often contemplated what would have happened if, during my service in World War I, a young German soldier and I had killed each other simultaneously and found ourselves together in the moments after death. I can't imagine either of us feeling resentment or even embarrassment. We might have laughed about it.

Someone might argue, "If we're allowed to condemn our enemies' actions, punish them, and even kill them, then what difference remains between Christian morality and the common view?" The difference is immense. Remember, we Christians believe that humans have an eternal existence. Therefore, what truly matters are the subtle marks or inclinations within the core, innermost part of the soul that will eventually shape it into a heavenly or hellish being. We may kill if necessary, but we must not hate or derive pleasure from hating. We may punish if necessary, but we must not enjoy it. In other words, that feeling of resentment and the desire for revenge within us must be eradicated. I don't mean that one can simply decide at a particular moment to never feel it again. It doesn't work that way. What I mean is that every time it resurfaces, day after day, year after year, throughout our lives, we must strike it down. It's hard work, but it's not impossible. Even as we punish or seek justice, we must strive to feel about our enemies as we feel about ourselves—wishing for their good, hoping that they can be healed and restored, if possible, in this world or the next. That's what loving them means: desiring their well-being, not feeling affectionate toward them, or pretending they are nice when they're not.

I admit that this means loving people who possess no lovable qualities. But then, do we ourselves have anything lovable about us? We love ourselves simply because we are ourselves.

God intends for us to love all individuals in the same way and for the same reason. He has given us the formula, already worked out in our own lives, to show us how it works. We must then proceed to apply this principle to all other individuals. Perhaps it becomes easier if we remember that this is exactly how God loves us. God doesn't love us for any pleasant or attractive qualities we think we possess but simply because we exist as beings called human. In reality, there's nothing else within us to love. We are creatures who often find pleasure in hatred, to the extent that giving it up is akin to giving up beer or tobacco.

The Great Sin

Now, I want to talk about a particular aspect of Christian morals that sets them apart from other moral systems. There is one vice that no one in the world is free from, a vice that everyone despises when they see it in others. Surprisingly, very few people, except Christians, ever admit to being guilty of this vice themselves. Additionally, non-Christians rarely show any mercy towards it when they see it in others. This vice is called Pride or Self-Conceit, and its opposite virtue, according to Christian morals, is called Humility. It's worth noting that when I discussed sexual morality, I mentioned that it is not the central focus of Christian morals. Well, now we have arrived at the center. According to Christian teachings, the ultimate vice, the greatest evil, is Pride. Other vices such as unchastity, anger, greed, drunkenness, and the like are relatively minor in comparison. It was through Pride that the devil became the devil, and Pride leads to every other vice. It represents a complete opposition to God.

Does this seem like an exaggeration? Take a moment to think about it. I mentioned earlier that the more pride one possesses, the more one dislikes pride in others. In fact, if you want to gauge your level of pride, ask yourself, "How much do I dislike it when others ignore me, belittle me, interrupt me, patronize me, or show off?" The truth is, each person's pride competes with the pride of others. It is because I want to be the center of attention at a party that I become annoyed when someone else takes that role. People in the same profession rarely get along.

Now, what you need to understand is that Pride is inherently competitive, unlike other vices that are competitive only incidentally. Pride does not derive pleasure from merely possessing something; it derives pleasure from having more of it than the next person. We say that people are proud of their wealth, intelligence, or physical attractiveness, but that's not entirely accurate. They are proud of being wealthier, smarter, or more attractive than others. If everyone became equally wealthy, intelligent, or good-looking, there would be nothing left to be proud of. It's the comparison that breeds pride — the satisfaction of being superior. Once the element of competition is removed, pride dissipates. That's why I say that Pride is essentially competitive in a way that other vices are not. The sexual impulse may lead two men to compete for the same woman, but that's merely incidental; they could just as easily desire different women. However, a proud person will take your partner away from you, not because they want them, but simply to prove to themselves that they are superior to you. Greed may lead individuals to compete when resources are scarce, but even when a proud person has more than they could ever need, they will still strive to acquire more in order to assert their power. Many of the world's evils, which people often attribute to greed or selfishness, are actually more deeply rooted in Pride.

Let's consider the role of money. Greed can certainly make a person desire money to afford a better house, luxurious vacations, or exquisite food and drinks. However, there comes a point when a person with an annual income of £10,000[24] becomes eager to earn £20,000 a year. It's not about the greed for more pleasure. £10,000 can provide all the luxuries that anyone can truly enjoy. It's Pride — the desire to be richer than

---

[24] Adjusted for inflation, that would be £175,000 ($US238,000) in 2023.

some other wealthy person and, more importantly, the desire for power. Yes, power is what Pride truly revels in. Nothing makes a person feel more superior to others than the ability to manipulate them like pawns on a chessboard. Why does a beautiful woman bring misery wherever she goes by collecting admirers? It's not because of her sexual instinct; such women are often sexually frigid[25]. It's Pride. Why do political leaders or entire nations continuously demand more and more? Again, it's Pride. Pride is inherently competitive, which is why it never ceases. As long as there is one person in the world who is more powerful, wealthier, or more intelligent than the proud person, that person becomes a rival and an enemy.

The Christians are correct. Pride has been the primary cause of misery in every nation and family throughout history. Other vices may occasionally bring people together; you can find camaraderie, jokes, and friendliness among drunkards or promiscuous individuals. But Pride always brings enmity[26] — it is enmity itself. And it is not only enmity towards other people but also enmity towards God.

When faced with God, we encounter something infinitely superior to ourselves in every aspect. Unless we know God in that way and, consequently, see ourselves as insignificant in comparison, we don't truly know God. As long as we are proud, we cannot know God. A proud person always looks down on things and people. And, of course, as long as you are looking down, you cannot see something that is above you.

This raises a troubling question. How is it that people who are clearly consumed by Pride can claim to believe in God and

---

[25] Frigid: abnormally averse to sexual intercourse, lacking warmth or ardor.

[26] Enmity: hatred, a feeling of hate.

consider themselves highly religious? Unfortunately, it means they are worshipping an imaginary God. They may theoretically admit their insignificance in the presence of this phantom God, but deep down, they imagine that He approves of them and considers them far better than ordinary people. They give a token display of humility to God and, in return, derive a substantial amount of Pride towards their fellow human beings. I suppose it was people of this sort that Christ had in mind when He said that some would preach about Him, perform miracles in His name, only to be told on the Day of Judgment that He never knew them. At any given moment, any one of us can fall into this trap. Fortunately, there is a test. Whenever we notice that our religious life makes us believe we are good, especially if we believe we are better than someone else, we can be certain that we are not influenced by God but by the devil. The genuine presence of God is characterized by either completely forgetting about ourselves or perceiving ourselves as small and flawed. It is better to forget about ourselves altogether.

It is a dreadful thing that the most insidious of vices can infiltrate the very core of our religious lives. However, there is a reason for this. Other, lesser vices arise when the devil exploits our animal nature. But Pride bypasses our animal nature entirely; it comes directly from Hell. It is purely spiritual and therefore much more subtle and deadly. Interestingly, Pride can sometimes be used to counteract simpler vices. In fact, teachers often appeal to a child's Pride, or what they call their self-respect, to encourage them to behave properly. Many individuals have overcome cowardice, lust, or anger by convincing themselves that such behaviors are beneath their dignity — by relying on Pride. The devil laughs. He is perfectly content to see you become chaste, brave, and self-controlled as long as he can establish the Dictatorship of Pride within you. He would be just as content to cure your chilblains[27] if, in return, he could give you cancer. Pride is like spiritual cancer; it corrodes any possibility of love, contentment, or even common sense.

Before I conclude, I want to clarify a few possible misunderstandings:

(1) Pleasure in receiving praise is not inherently Pride. When a child is praised for doing well in a lesson, or a woman's beauty is admired by her lover, or a saved soul hears Christ say, "Well done," it is natural to feel pleased, and rightfully so. The pleasure lies not in who you are but in the fact that you have pleased someone you wanted to please. The problem arises when you transition from thinking, "I have pleased them; everything is fine," to thinking, "I must be an exceptional person to have achieved this." The more delight you take in yourself and the less you delight in praise itself, the worse you become. When you find complete pleasure in yourself and no longer care about praise at all, you have reached rock bottom. That is why vanity, although it appears as the most visible form of Pride, is actually the least severe and most forgivable. Vain individuals desire excessive praise, applause, and admiration, but deep down, they still seek validation from others. They are, in essence, still human. The true, diabolical Pride emerges when you hold others in such contempt that you no longer care about their opinions. You may think, "Why should I care about the applause of that rabble? Their opinions are worthless. And even if their opinions had value, am I the kind of person who blushes with pleasure at a compliment, like an immature girl at her first dance? No, I am an integrated, mature individual. I have acted in accordance with my ideals, artistic conscience, family traditions, or personal characteristics. If the crowd approves, let

---

[27] Chilblains are small, itchy swellings on the skin that occur as a reaction to cold temperatures.

them. They mean nothing to me." In this way, thoroughgoing Pride can counteract vanity. As I mentioned before, the devil delights in "curing" a minor fault by introducing a significant one. We must strive not to be vain, but we should never rely on Pride to cure our vanity. It is better to endure the frying pan than leap into the fire.

(2) In English, we may say that a person is "proud" of their son, father, school, or regiment, and one may wonder if this type of "pride" is a sin. I believe it depends on what we precisely mean by "proud of." Often, in such expressions, "being proud of" implies "having a warm-hearted admiration for." Such admiration is far from being a sin. However, it might imply that the person in question displays an inflated sense of self-importance due to their distinguished father, association with a renowned institution, or membership in a prestigious regiment. That would certainly be a fault. Nevertheless, even in such cases, it would be preferable to have pride in something external to oneself rather than being solely proud of oneself. Loving and admiring something beyond ourselves is a step away from spiritual ruin, though we won't be truly well until we love and admire God more than anything else.

(3) We should not think that God forbids Pride because it offends Him, or that He demands Humility as a requirement for His own dignity—as if God Himself were proud. He is not concerned about His own dignity in the least. The point is that He wants you to know Him, to give yourself to Him fully. He and you are of such a nature that when you genuinely connect with Him, you will naturally become humble—humbly delighted, experiencing immense relief from discarding the absurd notions of your own dignity that have caused restlessness and unhappiness throughout your life. He seeks to make you humble to make this connection possible, to help you shed the ridiculous costume in which we all dress up and

parade around like foolish individuals. I wish I had made greater progress in humility myself because then I could better describe the relief and comfort that come from discarding the false self, with its incessant need for attention and affirmation. Even catching a glimpse of true humility, if only for a moment, is like quenching one's thirst with a drink of cold water in the desert.

(4) Finally, do not imagine that if you meet a genuinely humble person, they will fit the modern notion of humility — being greasy or overly obsequious[28], always claiming to be nobody. More likely, you will find them to be cheerful, intelligent individuals who take a genuine interest in what you have to say. If you happen to dislike such a person, it's probably because you feel a twinge of envy toward someone who seems to effortlessly enjoy life. A truly humble person is not preoccupied with humility; they are not preoccupied with themselves at all.

For anyone seeking to cultivate humility, I can offer what I believe is the first step: recognizing that you are proud. It is a significant step, and nothing can be done without it. If you believe that you are not conceited, then you are indeed very conceited.

---

[28] Obsequious: characterized by or showing servile obedience and excessive eagerness to please.

CHARITY

I mentioned earlier that there are four "Cardinal" virtues and three "Theological" virtues. The Theological virtues are Faith, Hope, and Charity. In this chapter, I will focus on Charity[29], which is also known as love in the Christian sense. Nowadays, Charity is often understood as giving to the poor, but its original meaning was much broader. Over time, giving to the poor became synonymous with Charity because it is one of the most evident expressions of love. Similarly, when people think of poetry, they often only think of rhyme, although poetry encompasses much more. Charity, in its Christian sense, is not an emotion but a state of the will. It is the same kind of love we naturally have for ourselves, which we must learn to extend to others.

In a previous chapter, I discussed Forgiveness as a part of Charity. Now, I want to add more to the understanding of Charity. First, let's clarify the meaning of the word itself. In Christian Love or Charity, affection or liking for someone is not the same as love itself. We may like or be fond of certain people and not others, and that is neither a sin nor a virtue, just a

---

[29] Charity: Greek *Agápe* (ἀγάπη), means "love: especially brotherly love, charity; the love of God for man and of man for God." Agápe is used in ancient texts to denote feelings for one's children and feelings for a spouse. Agápe is used by Christians to express the unconditional love of God for his children. This type of love was further explained by Thomas Aquinas as "to will the good of another."

personal preference. However, what matters is how we act upon those feelings. Our natural affection for others makes it easier to show charity towards them, so it is usually our duty to nurture our affections and like people as much as we can. It can be compared to encouraging our liking for exercise or healthy food—it is not the virtue of charity itself, but it aids in practicing it. Nevertheless, we must be vigilant to ensure that our liking for one person does not lead us to be uncharitable or unfair to others. Sometimes, our affection for someone may conflict with our charity towards that person. For example, a doting mother may be tempted by her natural affection to spoil her child, indulging her own emotions at the expense of the child's long-term happiness.

While it is generally beneficial to nurture our natural affections, it is incorrect to think that manufacturing affectionate feelings is the way to become charitable. Some people may have a naturally "cold" temperament, which is neither a sin nor a virtue but a misfortune for them, just like having poor digestion is a misfortune. However, it does not exempt them from the opportunity or duty to learn charity. The rule for all of us is simple: do not waste time questioning whether you "love" your neighbor; act as if you did. By behaving as if we love someone, we discover one of the great secrets of charity. When we act with love towards someone, we eventually come to genuinely love them. If we harm someone we dislike, we will find ourselves disliking them even more. Conversely, if we do them a good turn, we will find ourselves disliking them less. There is one exception, though. If we do someone a favor not out of a genuine desire to please God and practice the law of charity, but merely to show off or put them in our debt, hoping for gratitude, we will likely be disappointed. People can easily detect any form of showing off or patronage. However, whenever we do good to others simply because they are individuals, created by

God and desiring their own happiness as we desire ours, we will gradually learn to love them a little more or at least dislike them less.

Thus, although Christian charity may seem cold to those who are sentimental, and though it is distinct from affection, it eventually leads to affection. The difference between a Christian and a worldly person is not that the worldly person has affections or "likings" while the Christian has only "charity", the worldly person treats certain individuals kindly because they "like" them. In contrast, the Christian, striving to treat everyone kindly, finds themselves liking more and more people as they continue on this path, including people they couldn't have imagined liking at the beginning.

This same spiritual law works in the opposite direction as well. For example, the Germans initially mistreated the Jews because they hated them, but then they hated them even more because of the mistreatment. The crueller we are, the more we hate, and the more we hate, the more cruel we become. This vicious circle perpetuates the increase of both good and evil. That's why the small decisions we make every day are of immense importance. A seemingly minor good act today can be a strategic point captured, which months later allows us to achieve victories we never dreamed of. Likewise, a seemingly trivial indulgence in lust or anger today can lead to the loss of a crucial position from which the enemy can launch an otherwise impossible attack.

Some writers use the word charity to describe not only Christian love between human beings but also God's love for humanity and humanity's love for God. People often worry about the latter. They are told they should love God but cannot find such feelings within themselves. What should they do? The answer remains the same as before: act as if you did. Do not try to manufacture feelings. Instead, ask yourself, "If I were certain that I loved God, what would I do?" Once you find the answer, go and do it.

In general, contemplating God's love for us is safer than focusing on our love for Him. None of us can constantly have devout feelings, and even if we could, feelings are not what God primarily cares about. Christian love, whether directed towards God or other people, is a matter of the will. If we strive to do God's will, we are obeying the commandment to love the Lord our God. God will grant us feelings of love if He chooses to do so, but we cannot generate them ourselves, nor should we demand them as a right. The crucial thing to remember is that while our feelings may fluctuate, God's love for us remains constant. It is not weakened by our sins or indifference. Therefore, God's love is resolute in its determination to heal us from our sins, regardless of the cost to us or to Him.

HOPE

Hope is one of the virtues that is connected to our beliefs and faith. It means continually looking forward to the eternal world, and it's not a form of escapism or wishful thinking as some modern people may think. It's actually something that Christians are meant to do. However, this doesn't mean that we should neglect the present world. If we look at history, we'll see that the Christians who made the greatest impact on the world were the ones who focused on the next world. The Apostles themselves, who initiated the conversion of the Roman Empire, as well as the great figures who contributed to the development of the Middle Ages and the English Evangelicals who abolished the Slave Trade, all left their mark on Earth because their minds were occupied with Heaven. It is when Christians have stopped thinking about the other world that they have become ineffective in making a difference in this world.

The idea is that if we aim at Heaven, we will also attain earthly blessings. It may sound strange, but we can see a similar pattern in other aspects of life. Health, for example, is a great blessing, but if we make it our sole focus, we become obsessed and start imagining that there is something perpetually wrong with us. We are more likely to attain good health when we desire other things more, such as food, games, work, fun, and fresh air. Similarly, if our main goal is to save civilization, we will never truly achieve it. We need to learn to want something even more than the preservation of civilization.

For many of us, it is challenging to desire Heaven, except in terms of reuniting with our departed loved ones. This difficulty arises because we have not been trained to prioritize it. Our education often fixates our minds on this worldly existence. Another reason is that when the genuine desire for Heaven arises within us, we often fail to recognize it. Most people, if they truly examined their hearts, would realize that they want something profoundly and intensely that cannot be fulfilled in this world. This world offers various things that promise to satisfy our desires, but they never quite deliver on that promise. The longings we experience when we first fall in love, think about a foreign country, or engage in a passionate pursuit are longings that no marriage, travel, or learning can truly satisfy. I'm not referring only to unsuccessful marriages, disappointing vacations, or unfulfilling careers. Even the best possible experiences fall short of fulfilling that initial longing. There is always something that eludes us. I believe everyone can relate to this feeling.

There are two incorrect ways of dealing with this reality, and one correct way:

(1.) The Fool's Way: This person places the blame on external things. They spend their entire lives thinking that if only they tried another partner, went on a more extravagant vacation, or pursued a different hobby, they would finally find the elusive fulfillment they seek. Most bored, discontented, and wealthy people belong to this category. They continuously hop from one person to another, one continent to another, and one hobby to another, always convinced that the latest pursuit is the ultimate satisfaction they've been searching for, only to be disappointed once again.

(2.) The Way of the Disillusioned "Sensible Man": This person quickly concludes that the whole idea of finding ultimate satisfaction is an illusion. They might say, "Of course, when you're young, you feel like that. But as you get older, you give up chasing after an unattainable goal." So, they settle down, lower their expectations, and suppress the part of themselves that used to long for something more. This approach is better than the first one as it brings greater happiness and makes one less of a burden to society. However, it tends to make a person self-righteous and condescending toward what they perceive as "adolescent" desires. Despite these shortcomings, they can live a fairly comfortable life. This would be the ideal approach if human beings didn't live forever. But what if infinite happiness truly awaits us? What if we can actually reach the metaphorical rainbow's end? In that case, it would be a tragedy to realize too late, after death, that by stifling our innate capacity for enjoyment through so-called "common sense," we missed out on experiencing it.

(3.) The Christian Way: The Christian perspective acknowledges that creatures are not born with desires unless there is satisfaction available for those desires. A hungry baby craves food because food exists. A duckling wants to swim because water exists. Humans feel sexual desire because sex exists. If we find within ourselves a desire that no experience in this world can fulfill, the most reasonable explanation is that we were made for another world. The fact that none of our earthly pleasures can fully satisfy that longing doesn't mean that the universe is a deception. Instead, these pleasures are meant to awaken and hint at the reality of that something greater. In light of this understanding, we should be careful not to despise or be ungrateful for the blessings of this world. At the same time, we should never mistake these earthly pleasures for the true fulfillment they can only partially represent. We must keep alive within ourselves the desire for our true home, which we will only find after death. We must never allow this desire to be buried or diverted. Making it the primary focus of our lives to strive toward that otherworldly home and help others do the same is the right way to approach it.

There is no need to be concerned about those who try to ridicule the Christian hope of Heaven by saying that they don't want to spend eternity playing harps. Such people fail to understand books written for mature audiences, and therefore, their criticisms hold no weight. The imagery used in scripture, such as harps, crowns, and gold, is symbolic and attempts to express the inexpressible. Musical instruments are mentioned because they evoke feelings of ecstasy and infinity for many people in their present lives. Crowns represent the sharing of God's splendor, power, and joy by those united with Him in eternity. Gold is mentioned to convey the timeless nature of Heaven, as gold does not rust, and it signifies the preciousness of that realm. Those who interpret these symbols literally might as well think that when Christ told us to be like doves, He meant for us to lay eggs.

FAITH — PART ONE

I'll explain the concept of faith in everyday language. The term "faith" is used by Christians in two different ways, and I'll discuss each of them separately. In the first sense, faith means believing in or accepting the teachings of Christianity as true. This is a straightforward understanding of faith. However, what confuses people, as it used to confuse me, is why Christians consider faith in this sense to be a virtue. I used to wonder how believing or not believing a set of statements could be a moral issue. I thought that a rational person accepts or rejects a statement based on the evidence that seems good or bad to them. If someone is mistaken about the quality of the evidence, it doesn't mean they are morally wrong, but rather that they may not be very intelligent. And if someone recognizes the evidence as weak but still tries to believe in it, that would simply be foolish.

I still hold that view to some extent. However, what I failed to see then, and what many people still fail to see, is this: I assumed that once the human mind accepts something as true, it will automatically continue to regard it as true until some substantial reason arises to reconsider it. In other words, I believed that the human mind is completely governed by reason. But that's not the case. Let me give you an example. I know, based on solid evidence, that anesthesia doesn't suffocate me and that skilled surgeons don't start operating until I'm unconscious. Yet, when I'm lying on the operating table and they put that terrifying mask over my face, I experience a childish panic. I start thinking that I might suffocate and I fear they will begin cutting before I'm fully under. In other words, I lose my faith in anesthesia. It's not reason that diminishes my faith; on the contrary, my faith is rooted in reason. It's my imagination and emotions that create this internal struggle between faith and reason on one side, and emotion and imagination on the other.

You can observe similar instances of this phenomenon in everyday life. For example, a man may have solid evidence that a pretty girl he knows is a liar, untrustworthy, and unable to keep a secret. However, when he's with her, his mind loses faith in that knowledge, and he starts thinking, "Maybe she'll be different this time," only to make a fool of himself again and reveal something he shouldn't have. His senses and emotions have undermined his faith in what he truly knows to be true. Another example is a boy learning to swim. His reason tells him that a human body can float and swim in water, as he has seen many people do it. But the crucial question is whether he will continue to believe this when the instructor lets go of his hand and leaves him unsupported in the water. Will he maintain his belief or suddenly stop believing, succumbing to fear and sinking?

The same dynamics apply to faith in Christianity. I'm not asking anyone to accept Christianity if their reasoning indicates that the weight of evidence is against it. That's not the point where faith comes into play. However, if a person's reasoning leads them to believe that the weight of evidence supports Christianity, I can predict what will happen to them in the following weeks. There will come a moment when they receive bad news, face troubles, or live among non-believers, and suddenly their emotions will rise up, launching an assault on their faith. Alternatively, there will come a moment when they desire a woman, want to tell a lie, feel pleased with themselves, or spot an opportunity for unfair financial gain. In these moments, it would be convenient if Christianity were not true. And once again, their desires and emotions will launch an attack on their faith. I'm not referring to moments where genuine reasons against Christianity emerge. Those must be addressed separately. I'm talking about moments when a mere mood or impulse rises up against faith.

Now, faith, in the sense I'm using it here, is the skill of holding on to things your reason has accepted, despite the fluctuations in your moods. Moods will change, regardless of your rational perspective. I know this from personal experience. As a Christian, there are times when the whole belief system seems highly improbable to me. Yet, when I was an atheist, there were moments when Christianity appeared incredibly plausible. This clash between moods and our true selves is inevitable. That's why faith is an essential virtue. Without teaching your moods their place, you cannot be a grounded Christian or even a solid atheist. Instead, you become a creature constantly swaying back and forth, with your beliefs dependent on the weather and the state of your digestion. Therefore, it is crucial to cultivate the habit of faith.

The first step is to acknowledge that your moods change. The next step is to ensure that if you have accepted Christianity, you deliberately keep some of its key doctrines in your mind every day. This is why daily prayers, religious reading, and attending church are essential parts of the Christian life. We need constant reminders of what we believe because no belief, including Christianity, will automatically remain alive in our minds. It must be nurtured. In fact, if we were to examine a hundred people who have lost their faith in Christianity, I wonder how many of them would turn out to have reasoned their way out of it through honest arguments. Aren't most people simply drifting away?

Now, let's move on to faith in the second and higher sense, which is the most challenging aspect to explain. To approach it, let's revisit the topic of humility. As I mentioned earlier, the first step towards humility is to realize that one is proud. I want to add now that the next step is to make a genuine effort to practice the virtues taught by Christianity. Merely spending a week doing so is not sufficient. The initial week may go smoothly, but try six weeks. By that time, when you've seemingly fallen back entirely or even lower than where you started, you will discover certain truths about yourself. None of us truly understands how flawed we are until we earnestly strive to be good. There's a common misconception that good people don't comprehend the strength of temptation, but that's a blatant lie. Only those who actively resist temptation truly grasp its power. After all, you gauge the strength of an army by fighting against it, not by surrendering. You determine the strength of the wind by attempting to walk against it, not by lying down. Someone who succumbs to temptation within five minutes has no idea what it would have been like to resist an hour later. That's why morally compromised individuals, in a sense, know very little about their own wickedness. They've led sheltered lives by always giving in. We only uncover the strength of the evil impulse within us when we strive to combat it. Christ, being the only person who never yielded to temptation, is also the only one who fully comprehends its meaning — He is the only true realist. So, when a person has made these two discoveries — namely, that faith cannot be earned through a test or placed God in debt through a transaction — then God can truly begin His work. This is when real life begins. The person is now awake. And now, we can delve into discussing faith in the second sense.

FAITH — PART TWO

I want to emphasize something important that I hope everyone pays close attention to. If this chapter doesn't resonate with you or seems to address questions you haven't asked, feel free to disregard it entirely. There are certain aspects of Christianity that can be understood from an external perspective, even before becoming a Christian. However, there are many things that can only be comprehended after one has made some progress along the Christian journey. These aspects may appear practical, even though they may not seem that way initially. They provide guidance for navigating specific challenges and obstacles that arise on the journey, but their significance may only become apparent when a person reaches those points. So, if you encounter any statements in Christian writings that you don't understand, don't worry about it. Leave them be. There will come a day, perhaps years later, when the meaning will suddenly become clear. Trying to understand it now would only cause confusion.

Of course, everything I just said applies to me as much as anyone else. The topic I'm about to explain in this chapter may be beyond my own understanding. I might think I've grasped it when, in fact, I haven't. I can only ask knowledgeable Christians to observe carefully and point out any mistakes I make. For others, take what I say with a grain of salt. Consider it as something offered to help, not as an absolute truth.

Now, I want to discuss faith in the second sense, the higher sense. In the previous chapter, I mentioned that this type of faith arises after a person has sincerely attempted to practice the virtues taught by Christianity and discovered their inability to do so. They come to realize that even if they could succeed, they would only be returning to God what already belongs to Him. In other words, they recognize their own bankruptcy.

Here's the thing: what matters to God is not merely our actions. What matters is that we become the kind of creatures He intended us to be, creatures connected to Him in a specific way. I won't explicitly mention being connected to one another, as it is inherent. If we are rightly aligned with God, we will naturally be rightly aligned with our fellow creatures, just as the spokes of a wheel fall into place when properly fitted into the hub and rim. As long as a person views God as an examiner who has set a test or as the opposing party in a transaction, they haven't yet established the correct relationship with Him. They misunderstand their own nature and God's nature. They can't attain the right relationship until they recognize their own bankruptcy.

By "discovered," I mean genuinely discovering, not just repeating it without truly understanding. Of course, any child exposed to a certain type of religious education can quickly learn to say that we have nothing to offer God that isn't already His, and that we even fail to give Him what is already His. But I'm talking about truly experiencing and realizing this truth.

We can only truly discover our failure to keep God's law by trying our very hardest and still falling short. Unless we genuinely make the effort, whatever we say, deep down, we'll believe that if we try harder next time, we'll succeed in being completely good. Thus, in a sense, the path back to God involves moral effort — trying harder and harder. However, in another sense, it is not our striving that will ultimately bring us home. All this striving leads to a critical moment when we turn to God and say, "You must do this because I can't."[iii] I implore you not to start questioning yourself, wondering if you've reached that moment. Don't sit down and scrutinize your own mind to see if you're getting there. That will lead you astray. Often, when the most significant things occur in our lives, we don't immediately recognize what's happening. A person doesn't always think, "Oh, I'm growing up!" It's often only in retrospect that we realize what has happened and label it as "growing up." This even applies to simple matters. A person who anxiously monitors their sleep is likely to stay awake. Similarly, what I'm discussing may not happen to everyone in a sudden revelation, like it did for the apostle Paul or John Bunyan[30]. It may occur so gradually that one couldn't point to a specific hour or even year. What truly matters is the nature of the change itself, not how we feel while it's happening. It's a shift from being confident in our own efforts to a state of despair where we acknowledge our inability to accomplish anything for ourselves and surrender it to God.

I understand that the phrase "leave it to God" can be misinterpreted, but let it stand for now. Leaving it to God, as a Christian, means placing all our trust in Christ. We trust that Christ, in some way, will share with us His perfect human obedience from His birth to His crucifixion. He will make us more like Himself and rectify our deficiencies. In Christian terms, He shares His "sonship" with us, making us "Sons of God" like Himself. In Book IV, I will delve deeper into the meaning of those words. If you prefer, you can think of it this way: Christ offers something for nothing. In fact, He offers everything for nothing. In a sense, the entirety of the Christian life consists of accepting this remarkable offer. However, the challenge lies in reaching the point of recognizing that all our efforts are futile. What we may have desired is for God to tally

---

[30] John Bunyan authored The Pilgrim's Progress.

our good deeds and overlook our bad ones. Yet, you could say that such actions, done with the intention of purchasing Heaven, would not truly be good actions. They would merely be commercial transactions. On the other hand, some people have been accused of claiming that faith is all that matters. According to this view, if you have faith, your actions don't matter. They encourage indulging in sin and having a good time, with the belief that it won't make a difference in the end. The response to this fallacy is that if your so-called "faith" in Christ doesn't involve taking the slightest notice of what He says, then it's not genuine faith or trust in Him. It's merely intellectual acceptance of a theory about Him.

The Bible seems to settle this matter when it combines both aspects into one astonishing sentence. The first half says, "Work out your own salvation with fear and trembling," which implies that everything depends on us and our good actions. But the second half continues, "For it is God who works in you," which suggests that God does everything and we do nothing. Unfortunately, we encounter such paradoxes in Christianity. They puzzle us, but they shouldn't surprise us. You see, we are now attempting to understand and compartmentalize what God does and what humans do when we work together. However, this way of thinking eventually fails. God is not like another person working alongside us, where we can say, "He did this part, and I did that part." God is both inside us and outside us. Even if we could comprehend who did what, human language wouldn't be adequate to express it properly. Different churches express it differently in their attempts to articulate it. But you'll find that even those who emphasize the importance of good actions will still tell you that you need faith. Likewise, those who stress the significance of faith will urge you to do good deeds. That's as far as I'll go with this.

I believe all Christians would agree with me if I said that although Christianity initially seems to revolve around morality — duties, rules, guilt, and virtue — it leads us beyond all that, into something more profound. We catch a glimpse of a realm where people don't discuss those things, except perhaps as jokes. Everyone there is saturated with what we would call goodness, just as a mirror is filled with light. However, they don't label it as goodness or anything else. They aren't preoccupied with it; they're too busy gazing at the Source from which it emanates. Yet, this understanding is at the threshold where the road transcends our world. No one's eyes can see much further beyond that point. Many people's eyes can see farther than mine.

BOOK IV BEYOND PERSONALITY: FIRST STEPS IN THE DOCTRINE OF THE TRINITY

MAKING AND BEGETTING

Many people have advised me not to share what I'm going to reveal in this final book. They say, "The ordinary reader isn't interested in theology; give them practical religion instead." I've disregarded their advice because I don't think the ordinary reader is foolish. Theology is the study of God, and anyone who wants to contemplate God would appreciate having the clearest and most accurate understanding possible. You are not children, so why treat you as such?

I understand why some people are put off by theology. I recall an incident when I gave a talk to the Royal Air Force, and an experienced officer stood up and said, "I have no use for all that stuff. But mind you, I'm a religious man too. I know there's a God. I've felt His presence when I'm alone in the desert at night — the immense mystery. And that's precisely why I don't believe in all your neat little doctrines and formulas about Him. To someone who has encountered the real thing, they all seem trivial, pedantic, and unreal!"

In a way, I agreed with that man. I believe he had genuinely experienced God in the desert. And when he turned from that experience to Christian creeds, he probably felt like he was moving from something real to something less real. Similarly, if a person has stood on a beach and looked at the vast Atlantic Ocean, then later examines a map of the Atlantic, they are also transitioning from something real to something less real — a shift from observing actual waves to studying a colored piece of paper. However, there are two essential points to consider about the map. First, it is based on the collective experiences of countless individuals who have sailed the real Atlantic. The map integrates their diverse experiences, unlike your solitary glimpse from the beach. Second, if you want to go somewhere, the map is absolutely necessary. While walking on the beach and having your own glimpses may be more enjoyable than looking at a map, the map becomes indispensable when you want to reach America.

Theology is like that map. Simply learning and contemplating Christian doctrines, without going further, is less real and less exciting than the profound experiences my desert-dwelling friend had. Doctrines are not God; they are merely a form of guidance. But this guidance is based on the experiences of countless individuals who have genuinely connected with God — experiences far more profound and coherent than any fleeting thrills or pious sentiments you or I might have. And if you wish to progress, you must make use of that guidance. The truth is, if you don't engage with theology, it doesn't mean you have no ideas about God. It means you have a plethora of incorrect, confused, and outdated ideas. Many of the ideas about God presented as novelties today are actually concepts that genuine theologians explored centuries ago and dismissed. Believing in the popular religion of modern England (or North America) is a step backward, similar to believing the Earth is flat.

Let's examine the popular notion of Christianity: Jesus Christ was a great moral teacher, and if we follow His advice, we can establish a better social order and prevent future wars. Now, that statement is true to some extent. However, it reveals only a fraction of the whole truth about Christianity, and it has no practical significance on its own.

It's undoubtedly true that if we followed Christ's advice, we would live in a happier world. But we don't even need to go as far as Christ. If we followed the teachings of Plato, Aristotle, or Confucius, we would be much better off than we currently are. And then what? We've never truly followed the advice of the great teachers. Why would we start now? Why would we be more likely to follow Christ than any of the others? Is it because He is the best moral teacher? But that makes it even less likely that we would heed His teachings. If we can't grasp the fundamental lessons, is it likely that we would understand the most advanced one? If Christianity only offers one more piece of good advice, then it holds no real importance. There has been no shortage of good advice for the past four thousand years. A bit more makes no difference.

However, when you delve into authentic Christian writings, you discover that they discuss something entirely different from this popular religion. They assert that Christ is the Son of God (whatever that means). They proclaim that those who trust in Him can also become Sons of God (whatever that means). They declare that His death saved us from our sins (whatever that means).

One may argue that these statements are challenging. Christianity claims to reveal insights about another world, something beyond the tangible and perceptible realm. You might consider this claim false, but if it were true, the knowledge it imparts would inevitably be difficult—just as modern physics is difficult for the same reason.

Now, the aspect of Christianity that shocks us the most is the notion that by aligning ourselves with Christ, we can "become Sons of God." One might ask, "Aren't we already Sons of God? Isn't the fatherhood of God one of the central Christian ideas?" Well, in a certain sense, we may indeed be Sons of God already. God has given us life, loves us, cares for us, and in that way, resembles a father. However, when the Bible speaks of our "becoming" Sons of God, it obviously refers to something different. And this brings us to the heart of theology.

One of the creeds states that Christ is the Son of God, "begotten, not created," and it adds, "begotten by His Father before all worlds." Please understand that this has nothing to do with the fact that Jesus, as a man, was born to a virgin. We are not currently discussing the Virgin Birth. Instead, we are contemplating something that occurred before the existence of Nature, before time itself. "Before all worlds," Christ was begotten, not created. What does that mean?

We don't frequently use the words "begetting" or "begotten" in modern English, but everyone still understands their meaning. To beget is to become the father of, while to create is to make. The difference lies here: when you beget, you bring forth something of the same nature as yourself. A man begets human babies, a beaver begets little beavers, and a bird begets eggs that hatch into little birds. But when you make, you produce something different from yourself. A bird builds a nest, a beaver constructs a dam, and a man creates a radio—or perhaps something more akin to himself, like a statue. If a skilled sculptor carves a statue that closely resembles a man, it may be incredibly lifelike. However, it is not a real man; it merely looks like one. It cannot breathe or think, lacking the vitality of life.

That is the first concept we need to grasp. What God begets is God, just as what a man begets is a man. What God creates is not God, just as what a man makes is not a man. This is why humans are not Sons of God in the same sense as Christ. We may share certain similarities with God, but we are not of the same essence. We are more like statues or images of God.

A statue has the shape of a man but lacks life. Similarly, man possesses (in a sense I will explain) the "shape" or likeness of

God, but lacks the kind of life that God possesses. Let's first consider man's resemblance to God. Everything God has created bears some resemblance to Him. Space resembles God in its vastness, although the greatness of space differs from God's greatness. It serves as a symbol or representation of that greatness in non-spiritual terms. Matter resembles God in its energy, although physical energy is distinct from the power of God. The world of plants resembles God because it is alive, and He is the "living God." However, this biological life is not the same as the life within God; it is merely a symbolic or shadowy representation of it. When we look at animals, we observe additional resemblances alongside biological life. For example, the intense activity and fertility of insects represent a rudimentary reflection of God's ceaseless activity and creativity. In higher mammals, we find the beginnings of instinctual affection. It is not the same as the love that exists in God, but it bears some similarity — similar to how a flat piece of paper with a drawing can resemble a landscape. As we reach the pinnacle of the animal kingdom with man, we encounter the most complete resemblance to God that we are aware of (although there might be creatures in other worlds who resemble God more than we do, but we lack knowledge about them). Man not only lives but also loves and reasons — biological life reaches its zenith in him.

However, what man lacks in his natural state is spiritual life — a higher and distinct form of life that exists in God. We use the same word, "life," for both, but assuming that they are the same would be akin to believing that the vastness of space and God's greatness are identical. In reality, the distinction between biological life and spiritual life is crucial, so I will assign them two separate names. The biological life that we inherit through nature, which like everything else in nature tends to deteriorate and decay, requires constant sustenance from nature in the form of air, water, food, and so on—I will call this "Bios." The spiritual life that exists in God from eternity, the life that created the entire natural universe, I will call "Zoe." Bios[31] does bear a shadowy resemblance to Zoe[32], but it is akin to the resemblance between a photograph and a place or a statue and a man. If a person were to transition from Bios to Zoe, they would undergo a profound transformation, similar to a statue changing from carved stone to a living human being.

And that is precisely what Christianity is about. This world is akin to a sculptor's workshop, and we are the statues. There is a rumor circulating in the workshop that some of us will one day come to life.

---

[31] Bios: refers to concepts and phenomena related to living organisms or the study of life itself

[32] Zoe: a female given name: from a Greek word meaning "[spirit of] life."

THE THREE-PERSONAL GOD

In the previous chapter, we discussed the distinction between begetting and making. A man begets a child, but he only creates a statue. God begets Christ, but He only creates human beings. However, this explanation only touches on one aspect of God, namely, that what God the Father begets is God—a being of the same kind as Himself. It is somewhat similar to a human father begetting a human son, but not entirely. So let me try to explain a bit further.

Many people today claim, "I believe in God, but not in a personal God." They believe that the mysterious force underlying everything must be more than just a person. Interestingly, Christians agree with them. However, Christians are the only ones who offer an idea of what a being beyond personality might be like. Other people who claim that God is beyond personality actually perceive Him as something impersonal, something less than a person. If you are searching for something super-personal, something more than a person, then it is not a matter of choosing between the Christian concept and other ideas. The Christian idea is the only one available.

Similarly, some people believe that after this life, or perhaps after multiple lives, human souls will be "absorbed" into God. But when they attempt to explain what they mean, it seems as though they imagine our absorption into God as one material substance being absorbed into another. They describe it as a drop of water blending into the sea. However, in that case, the drop ceases to exist. If that is what happens to us, then being absorbed is equivalent to ceasing to exist. Only Christians have an understanding of how human souls can be incorporated into the life of God and yet retain their individuality — actually becoming more fully themselves than before.

I mentioned earlier that theology is practical. The very purpose of our existence is to be drawn into the life of God in this manner. Misconceptions about what that life entails can make it more challenging. Now, I ask you to pay close attention for a few moments.

You are aware that in space, movement can occur in three ways: left or right, backward or forward, up or down. Every direction is either one of these three or a combination of them. These are called the three dimensions. Now, consider this: if you were restricted to one dimension, you could only draw a straight line. With two dimensions, you could create a shape, like a square, which consists of four straight lines. Now, take it a step further. In three dimensions, you can construct a solid object, such as a cube, resembling a dice or a lump of sugar. And a cube is made up of six squares.

Do you understand the point I'm making? A world confined to one dimension would consist of straight lines. In a two-dimensional world (like a flat sheet of paper), you would still have straight lines, but many lines would form a shape. In a three-dimensional world, shapes would still exist, but many shapes would constitute a solid object. In other words, as we progress to more complex and tangible levels, we don't leave behind what we encountered in simpler levels. We retain those elements but combine them in new ways — ways that we couldn't imagine if we only knew the simpler levels.

The same principle applies to the Christian understanding of God. The human level is straightforward and somewhat limited. At this level, one person is one individual, and any two persons are two separate entities — similar to how, in two dimensions, one square represents one shape, and any two squares are two distinct figures. On the divine level, personalities still exist, but they are combined in new ways that we, who don't reside on that level, cannot envision. In God's dimension, so to speak, there exists a being who is three Persons while remaining one Being — just as a cube consists of six squares yet remains a single cube. Of course, we cannot fully grasp the nature of such a being, just as we couldn't properly conceive a cube if we were limited to perceiving only two dimensions in space. However, we can have a faint notion of it. And when we do, we begin to grasp, albeit faintly, something super-personal — something more than a person. It is something we couldn't have guessed, yet once we are informed, we almost feel as if we should have been able to guess it because it harmonizes so well with everything we already know.

You might wonder, "If we can't imagine a three-personal Being, what's the point of discussing it?" Well, there is no point in merely talking about Him. What truly matters is being drawn into that three-personal life, and that can commence at any time — right now, if you wish.

Allow me to explain further. When an ordinary Christian kneels down to pray, they are seeking to connect with God. But if they are a Christian, they know that the inner prompting to pray is also God — a divine presence within them. They are aware that their genuine knowledge of God comes through Christ, the Man who is God. They recognize that Christ stands beside them, assisting them in prayer, even praying[33] on their behalf. Do you see what is happening here? God is both the entity to whom they are praying — the ultimate goal they are striving for — and the presence within them, driving them forward as the

---

[33] Interceding.

motivating force. God also serves as the path or bridge leading them to that goal. Thus, the complete threefold life of the three-personal Being is actively unfolding in an ordinary bedroom where an ordinary individual is engaged in prayer. The person is being caught up into a higher form of life, what I referred to as Zoe or spiritual life. They are being drawn into God by God, all the while retaining their individual identity.

And that is how theology originated. People already had a vague understanding of God. Then, a man claimed to be God, and yet he was not the type of man one could dismiss as a lunatic. He made them believe in Him. They encountered Him again after witnessing His crucifixion. Later, once they had formed a small society or community, they experienced God within them—guiding them, empowering them to accomplish things they were incapable of before. Upon contemplating all these occurrences, they arrived at the Christian definition of the three-personal God.

This definition is not something they fabricated. Theology is, in a sense, a form of experimental knowledge. The simple religions are the ones that are invented. When I say that theology is an experimental science "in a sense," I mean that it shares similarities with other experimental sciences in certain aspects, but not in all. If you are a geologist studying rocks, you must actively seek out the rocks. They won't come to you, and if you go to them, they cannot evade you. The initiative lies entirely on your side. They cannot assist or hinder you. Now, consider a higher stage: suppose you wish to study wild animals and take photographs of them in their natural habitats. That differs from studying rocks. Wild animals won't come to you; they can run away from you. Unless you remain very quiet, they will elude you. Here, there is a tiny trace of initiative on their part.

Now, take it one step further: imagine you want to truly know a human person. If that person is determined not to let you get to know them, you will never succeed. You must earn their trust. In this case, the initiative is equally divided — it takes two to establish a friendship.

When it comes to knowing God, the initiative rests with Him. If He doesn't reveal Himself, nothing you do will enable you to find Him. Moreover, He reveals Himself to some people more than others — not because He has favorites, but because it is impossible for Him to reveal Himself fully to someone whose mind and character are in the wrong state[v]. Just as sunlight, though impartial, cannot be reflected clearly in a dusty mirror compared to a clean one.

We can view this from another perspective: while other sciences employ external instruments (such as microscopes and telescopes), the instrument through which you perceive God is your whole self. And if a person's self is not kept clean and bright, their glimpse of God will be blurred — like viewing the Moon through a dirty telescope. That's why nations steeped in horrors possess dreadful religions — they have been looking at God through a tainted lens.

God can reveal Himself as He truly is only to authentic individuals. This means not only those who are individually righteous, but also those who are united in a community, loving one another, assisting one another, and showing God to one another. This is precisely how God intended humanity to function — like members of a band playing together or organs comprising a single body.

Hence, the most suitable instrument for comprehending God is the entire Christian community, waiting for Him collectively. Christian brotherhood, so to speak, is the technical equipment for this science — the laboratory apparatus. That's why those who periodically emerge with their own invented and simplified religions, posing as substitutes for the Christian tradition, are simply wasting time. It's akin to an individual armed with an old pair of binoculars trying to correct all the real astronomers. They might be intelligent, perhaps even more so than some astronomers, but they aren't giving themselves a fair chance. And two years later, everyone has forgotten about them, while genuine scientific inquiry persists.

If Christianity were something we made up, we could certainly make it easier. However, it isn't. We can't compete, in terms of simplicity, with people who fabricate religions. How could we? We are dealing with reality. Of course, anyone can be simple if they don't have to contend with facts that complicate matters.

TIME AND BEYOND TIME

Some people may find this chapter to be an unnecessary complication, while others may find it helpful. If you belong to the first group, feel free to skip this chapter and move on to the next.

I want to address a difficulty that some people have with the concept of prayer, especially in relation to the idea of God listening attentively to millions of people all at once. The main issue here is the idea of God fitting too many things into a single moment of time.

In our own lives, time passes moment by moment, with each moment quickly replaced by the next. We tend to assume that this is how time works for everything, including the universe and God Himself. However, there are scholars who disagree with this view. Theologians first introduced the idea that some things exist outside of time, and now philosophers and scientists are exploring the same concept.

It is highly likely that God exists outside of time. His life does not consist of moments following one another. If a million people pray to Him at the same time, He doesn't have to listen to each of them within that particular moment we call "the same time." For God, every moment, from the beginning of the world to the present, is always the present moment. He has all of eternity to listen to a split second of prayer from a pilot as their plane crashes.

I understand that this concept is difficult to grasp. Let me provide an imperfect analogy to help you understand. Imagine I am writing a novel, and I write, "Mary laid down her work; next moment came a knock at the door!" For Mary, who exists within the imaginary time of my story, there is no interval between putting down her work and hearing the knock. However, as the author, I do not exist within that imaginary time at all. Between writing the first and second parts of that sentence, I might sit down for three hours and think deeply about Mary. I can think about Mary as if she were the only character in the book for as long as I want, and the hours I spend thinking about her won't be accounted for in Mary's time within the story.

While this analogy is not perfect, it provides a glimpse of the truth. God is not rushed along in the time-stream of our universe, just as an author is not rushed along in the imaginary time of their novel. He has infinite attention for each one of us and doesn't have to deal with us as en masse. When you are in the presence of God, it's as if you are the only being He has ever created. When Christ died, He died for you individually, as if you were the only person in the world.

The analogy I provided breaks down in one aspect. In the analogy, the author transitions from one time-series (the novel) to another (the real world). However, I believe that God doesn't exist within a time-series at all. His life is not divided into moments like ours; it is eternal and encompasses all time. He is fully present in every moment.

To help you grasp this idea, imagine time as a straight line that we travel along. God is like the entire page on which the line is drawn. We experience different parts of the line one by one, leaving one moment behind to reach the next. God, from above or beyond, contains the entire line and sees it all.

Understanding this concept can resolve some apparent difficulties in Christianity. One objection I had before becoming a Christian was how the universe could continue while God, in human form, was a baby or asleep. I struggled with the idea of God being both the omniscient being who knows everything and a man asking His disciples, *"Who touched me?"*[34] The difficulty lies in thinking that Christ's life as God existed within our concept of time and that His life as the human Jesus in Palestine was a brief period within that time. But this perspective might not align with the actual facts. You can't fit Christ's earthly life into a time-based relationship with His life as God, which transcends all space and time. It's a timeless truth that human nature, with its experiences of weakness, sleep, and ignorance, is somehow included in God's divine life. From our viewpoint, this human life in God corresponds to a specific period in our world's history (from A.D. 1 to the Crucifixion). We imagine it as a period in God's existence, but God has no history. His reality is complete and unbounded. We hope that we, too, won't be confined to such limited rationing of time.

Another challenge arises when we consider that believers in God often believe He knows what we will do in the future. But if He already knows our actions, how can we be free to do otherwise? Once again, this difficulty arises from thinking that God progresses along the same timeline as us, but with the added ability to see ahead. However, if God exists outside and above the timeline, then what we perceive as "tomorrow" is visible to Him in the same way as what we perceive as "today." All days are "Now" for Him. He doesn't remember what we did yesterday; He simply sees it because, although we have left yesterday behind, He hasn't. He doesn't "foresee" our actions tomorrow; He simply sees them because, although tomorrow

---

[34] The Bible: Mark 5:30-32

isn't here for us yet, it is for Him. God never restricts our freedom by knowing our actions in advance. He already sees our actions as we perform them because He transcends time.

This idea has brought me a great deal of understanding. If it doesn't resonate with you, feel free to disregard it. It's considered a "Christian idea" because many wise Christians have embraced it, and it doesn't contradict Christianity. However, it isn't explicitly stated in the Bible or the creeds. You can be a perfectly good Christian without accepting or even considering this concept.

GOOD INFECTION

L et's start this chapter by picturing two books lying on a table, one on top of the other. The bottom book, let's call it A, is supporting the top book, B, and keeping it from touching the table. The position of A determines the position of B. Are you following? Now, let's imagine that these two books have been in that position for eternity. In that case, B's position would always be a result of A's position. However, A's position (being underneath) wouldn't have existed before B's position. The effect doesn't come after the cause. Usually, results do come after their causes, like when you eat a cucumber and then experience indigestion. But that's not always the case with all causes and effects. I'll explain why this is important in a moment.

In the previous chapter, I mentioned that God is a being who contains three persons while remaining one being, just as a cube contains six squares while remaining one object. But when I try to explain how these persons are connected, I have to use words that may make it seem as if one of them existed before the others. We call the first person the Father and the second person the Son. We say that the Father begets or produces the Son because what He produces is of the same kind as Himself. So, the term "Father" is appropriate. Unfortunately, it may imply that He was there first, just like a human father exists before his son. But that's not the case. There is no before and after in this context. That's why I've taken some time to explain how one thing can be the source or cause of another without being there before it. The Son exists because the Father exists, but there was never a time when the Father produced the Son.

Perhaps the best way to think about it is this: imagine the two books I mentioned earlier. When I asked you to picture them, you used your imagination, and as a result, you had a mental image. Clearly, your act of imagining caused the mental picture to appear. But that doesn't mean you first did the imagining and then got the picture. The moment you started imagining, the picture was there. Your will kept the picture in front of you the entire time. The act of will and the picture began and ended simultaneously. If there were a being who had always existed and had always been imagining something, their act of imagination would always produce a mental picture. In this case, the picture would be as eternal as the act of imagination itself.

Similarly, we should think of the Son as constantly emanating from the Father, like light from a lamp, heat from a fire, or thoughts from a mind. The Son is the self-expression of the Father, what the Father has to say. There was never a time when the Father wasn't expressing Himself. However, you may have noticed that these analogies, such as light or heat, make it sound as if the Father and Son are two things rather than two persons. In the end, the New Testament's depiction of a Father and a Son turns out to be more accurate than any substitutes we might come up with. This is what always happens when we deviate from the words of the Bible. It's fine to depart from them momentarily to clarify a specific point, but we must always return to them. God knows how to describe Himself far better than we do. He knows that Father and Son is the closest resemblance to the relationship between the First and Second Persons. Most importantly, this relationship is one of love. The Father takes delight in the son, and the Son looks up to the Father.

Now, let's consider the practical significance of all this. Many people like to repeat the Christian statement that "God is love." However, they often fail to realize that the words "God is love" hold no real meaning unless God contains at least two persons. Love is something one person feels for another person. If God were a solitary individual, then before the world was created, He couldn't have experienced love. Of course, what these people usually mean when they say "God is love" is something quite different. They actually mean "Love is God." They believe that our feelings of love, wherever and however they arise, and the results they produce, should be highly regarded. Perhaps they should, but that's quite different from what Christians mean by the statement "God is love." Christians believe that the dynamic and living activity of love has existed within God for all eternity and has brought everything else into being.

In fact, this is perhaps the most significant difference between Christianity and other religions. In Christianity, God is not a static entity, not even just a person, but a dynamic and vibrant activity—a life, almost like a drama. You could even think of it as a dance, if you don't find it disrespectful. The union between the Father and the Son is so alive and real that this union itself is also a person—the Third of the three persons who are God.

This third person is called, in technical terms, the Holy Spirit or the "spirit" of God. Don't be surprised if you find this person somewhat vague or shadowy in your mind compared to the other two. There's a reason for that. In the Christian life, you're not typically looking directly at the Holy Spirit; rather, He is always working through you. If you think of the Father as something "out there" in front of you and the Son as someone standing at your side, helping you pray and transforming you into another child of God, then you should think of the third person as something inside you or behind you. For some people, it might be easier to start with the third person and work backward. God is love, and that love works through human beings, especially through the entire community of Christians. But this spirit of love has always existed eternally as a love shared between the Father and the Son.

And now, why does all of this matter? It matters more than anything else in the world. The entire dance, drama, or pattern of this three-personal life is meant to be played out in each one of us. In other words, each one of us must enter that pattern and take our place in that dance. There is no other path to the happiness for which we were created. Just like good and bad things are contagious, you know, through some kind of infection, if you want to get warm, you have to stand near a fire; if you want to get wet, you have to get into water. If you desire joy, power, peace, and eternal life, you must get close to or even participate in the very source of those qualities. They are not prizes that God can simply hand out to anyone. They are a tremendous fountain of energy and beauty that gushes forth from the very center of reality. If you are close to it, you'll feel the spray; if you are distant, you'll remain dry. Once a person is united with God, how could they not live forever? Conversely, once a person is separated from God, what can they do but wither and die?

But how can we be united with God? How is it possible for us to partake in this three-personal life? Do you remember what I said in Chapter II about begetting and making? We are not begotten by God; we are only made by Him. In our natural state, we are not children of God; we are merely like statues. We do not possess Zoe, which is spiritual life; we only have Bios, which is biological life that eventually deteriorates and dies. Now, the entire offer that Christianity presents to us is this: if we allow God to have His way, we can share in the life of Christ. If we do, we will also become children of God. We will love the Father as He does, and the Holy Spirit will manifest within us. Christ came to this world and became a human being in order to spread His kind of life to other human beings through what I call "good infection." Every Christian is meant to become a reflection of Christ. The entire purpose of becoming a Christian is nothing less than this.

THE OBSTINATE TOY SOLDIERS

The purpose of the Son of God becoming a human being was to enable human beings to become children of God. We can only speculate on how things would have worked if the human race had never rebelled against God and joined the enemy. Maybe every person would have been "in Christ," sharing the life of the Son of God from the moment of their birth. Perhaps the natural life would have seamlessly transformed into the spiritual life right away. But that's just speculation. What matters is the way things work now.

Currently, the two types of life are not only different (they would always have been different), but they are also in direct opposition. The natural life within each of us is self-centered. It craves attention, admiration, and the exploitation of other lives and the entire universe. Above all, it wants to be left alone, far away from anything superior, stronger, or higher that might make it feel inferior. It fears the spiritual realm, just like people who have grown accustomed to being dirty fear taking a bath. And in a sense, it's justified. It knows that if the spiritual life takes hold of it, all its self-centeredness and self-will would be annihilated, and it will do everything in its power to avoid that.

Did you ever imagine as a child how amazing it would be if your toys could come to life? Now, suppose you could truly bring them to life, turning a tin soldier into a real little man. That would require transforming the tin into flesh. But what if the tin soldier didn't like it? He wouldn't be interested in becoming flesh; all he would see is that his tin form is being ruined. He would think that you're killing him and would do everything possible to resist the transformation.

I don't know what you would have done in that situation with the tin soldier. But I can tell you what God did with us. The Second Person of the Godhead, the Son, became a human being Himself. He was born into the world as an actual man—a real man with specific physical characteristics, speaking a particular language, and having a specific weight. The Eternal Being, who knows everything and created the entire universe, not only became a man but also became a baby, and even earlier, a fetus inside a woman's body. If you want to grasp the concept, imagine how it would feel to become a slug or a crab.

As a result of this, there was now one man who truly embodied what all human beings were meant to be. This man allowed the natural life derived from his mother to be completely and perfectly transformed into the begotten life. The natural human creature within him merged entirely with the divine Son. In this instance, humanity had, so to speak, reached its full potential and entered into the life of Christ. And because the primary difficulty for us lies in the fact that the natural life must be, in a sense, "killed," He chose a human existence that involved suppressing His human desires at every turn—poverty, misunderstanding from His own family, betrayal by a close friend, ridicule and mistreatment by the authorities, and ultimately execution through torture. And then, after being killed in this manner every day, the human aspect within Him, because it was united with the divine Son, came back to life. The Man in Christ rose again: not only the God. That is the crux of the matter. For the first time, we witnessed a real man—a tin soldier, a real tin soldier, just like the others, had come vibrantly and fully alive.

However, this is where my illustration about the tin soldier falls short. In the case of real toy soldiers or statues, if one were to come to life, it wouldn't affect the others in any way. They are all separate entities. But human beings are not. They appear separate because we see them walking around individually. However, we are designed to perceive only the present moment. If we could see the past, it would look different. There was a time when every person was part of their mother, and even earlier, part of their father, and their parents were part of their grandparents. If we could see humanity unfold in time as God sees it, it wouldn't resemble a collection of separate entities scattered about. It would resemble a single, interconnected, and complex organism, much like a vast, intricate tree. Each individual would be interconnected with every other individual. And not only that, individuals are not truly separate from God any more than they are from one another. Every man, woman, and child all over the world is currently feeling and breathing because God, so to speak, is keeping them alive.

Therefore, when Christ became a man, it was not as if you could become one specific tin soldier. It's more like something that perpetually affects the entire human race suddenly begins to impact the entirety of humanity in a new way from one focal point. From that moment onward, the impact spreads throughout all of mankind. It makes a difference to people who lived before Christ as well as those who came after Him. It even affects those who have never heard of Him. It's comparable to dropping a single drop of a substance into a glass of water, instantly giving it a new taste or color. But, of course, none of these illustrations can perfectly capture the truth. Ultimately, God is entirely unique, and His actions are unlike anything else. We can hardly expect it to be otherwise.

So, what difference has He made to all of humanity? The difference is this: the process of becoming a child of God, of transforming from a created entity into a begotten entity, of transitioning from temporary biological life to timeless spiritual life, has already been accomplished for us. Humanity is already "saved" in principle. As individuals, we need to appropriate that salvation. But the most challenging part — the part we could never have done on our own — has been done for us. We don't have to strive to ascend to spiritual life through our own efforts; it has already descended upon the human race. If we simply open ourselves up to the one Man in whom this new life was fully present, and who, despite being God, is also a genuine human being, He will bring about the transformation in us and for us. Remember what I mentioned earlier about "good infection." One person from our own race possesses this new life. If we draw near to Him, we will catch it from Him.

Of course, you can express this in various ways. You can say that Christ died for our sins. You can say that the Father has forgiven us because Christ accomplished what we should have done. You can say that we are cleansed by the blood of the Lamb. You can say that Christ has conquered death. All of these statements are true. If some of them don't resonate with you, leave them aside and focus on the ones that do. And no matter what, don't start quarreling with others just because they use different expressions than you do.

TWO NOTES

To avoid any misunderstandings, I want to address two points that emerged from the previous chapter.

(1) One critic asked me why, if God wanted sons instead of "toy soldiers," He didn't simply beget many sons from the beginning rather than creating toy soldiers and then bringing them to life through a difficult and painful process. Part of the answer to this question is relatively straightforward, while another part is likely beyond human comprehension. The easy part is this: the process of transforming from a creature into a son wouldn't have been difficult or painful if the human race hadn't turned away from God long ago. They were able to do so because God granted them free will, which was necessary for genuine love and the potential for infinite happiness. The difficult part is contemplating the notion of multiple "Sons of God." When we ask if there could have been many, we find ourselves grappling with a profound mystery. Do the words "could have been" have any meaning at all when applied to God? It is possible to say that a particular finite thing "could have been" different from what it is, as it would have been if something else had been different, and so on. (For instance, the letters on this page would have been red if the printer had used red ink, and the printer would have used red ink if instructed to do so.) However, when discussing God — referring to the fundamental and unalterable Reality upon which all other facts depend — it is nonsensical to inquire if It could have been otherwise. It simply is what It is, and that's the end of the

matter. Moreover, setting aside this point, I encounter a challenge in even conceiving the idea of the Father begetting many sons for all eternity. For them to be considered many, they would have to be somehow different from one another. Two pennies may have the same shape, so how can they be considered two? They occupy different spaces and contain different atoms. In other words, to perceive them as distinct, we need to introduce space, matter, and ultimately, "Nature" or the created universe. I can grasp the distinction between the Father and the Son without invoking space or matter because one begets and the other is begotten. The Father's relationship with the Son is not the same as the Son's relationship with the Father. However, if there were multiple sons, they would all be related to one another and to the Father in the same way. How would they differ from one another? Initially, this difficulty may not be apparent. We might believe we can conceive the notion of several "sons." Yet, upon closer examination, I realize that the idea seemed possible only because I vaguely imagined them as human forms gathered together in some kind of space. In other words, although I claimed to contemplate something existing before any universe was created, I was actually smuggling in the image of a universe and placing that something within it. When I refrain from doing so and attempt to truly envision the Father begetting many sons "before all worlds," I find that I'm not truly thinking of anything. The idea dissolves into mere words. (Was the created Nature—space, time, and matter—established specifically to make manyness feasible? Could there be no other means of having numerous eternal spirits except by first creating multiple natural beings within a universe and subsequently spiritualizing them? However, all of this remains speculative.)

(2) The notion that the entire human race is, in a sense, a single entity—a vast organism akin to a tree—should not be mistaken

for the idea that individual differences don't matter or that real people, such as Tom, Toby, and Kate, are somehow less significant than collective entities like classes or races. In fact, these two ideas are opposites. Parts of a unified organism can be vastly dissimilar, while things that are not part of the same organism can be very similar. Six nickels, for example, are separate yet alike, whereas my nose and my lungs are quite distinct but are only alive because they are components of my body, sharing its common life. Christianity regards individuals not merely as members of a group or items on a list but as organs within a body—each unique, contributing in a way that no other organ can. So, when you feel the inclination to mold your children, students, or even your neighbors into carbon copies of yourself, remember that God likely didn't intend for them to be that way. You and they are distinct organs meant to fulfill different purposes. On the other hand, when you're tempted to disregard someone else's troubles because they're "none of your business," remember that although they are different from you, they are part of the same organism as you. Forgetting this shared belongingness may lead to individualism. Similarly, if you seek to suppress differences and enforce uniformity among people, you may drift toward totalitarianism. However, a Christian should not embrace either totalitarianism or individualism.

I sense a strong desire in both you and me to determine which of these two errors is worse. This is the devil's doing. He always introduces errors into the world as opposing pairs. Moreover, he encourages us to spend excessive time contemplating which error is more severe. Can you see why? He relies on our particular aversion to one error to gradually draw us toward the opposite one. But let us not be deceived. Our focus should be fixed on the ultimate goal, proceeding straight between both errors. We have no other concern but that, with either of them.

LET'S PRETEND

Let me start by sharing two stories with you. The first story is Beauty and the Beast. You're familiar with it. The girl had to marry a monster for some reason, and she did. She kissed him as if he were a man, and to her relief, he actually transformed into a man, and everything turned out well. The second story is about someone who wore a mask that made them look much nicer than they actually were. They had to wear the mask for a year, and when they finally took it off, their own face had changed to match the mask, making them truly beautiful. What started as a disguise became reality. These stories, although imaginative, can help illustrate my point in this chapter. Until now, I've been explaining facts — what God is and what He has done. Now I want to discuss practical matters — what do we do next? How does all this theology impact our lives? It can start making a difference right now. If you've been interested enough to read this far, then you're probably interested enough to give prayer a try[v], and most likely, you'll say the Lord's Prayer.

The first words of the Lord's Prayer are "Our Father." Do you understand what those words mean? They mean, to put it frankly, that you are considering yourself a child of God. In other words, you're pretending to be like Christ. If you prefer, you can see it as an act of pretending. Because, of course, the moment you realize the meaning of those words, you also realize that you are not truly a son of God. You're not behaving like the Son of God, whose will and interests are in harmony with those of the Father. Instead, you're a bundle of self-centered fears, hopes, greed, jealousy, and self-conceit, all destined for death. So, in a way, pretending to be like Christ may seem audacious. But the strange thing is that He has instructed us to do it.

Why? What's the point of pretending to be something you're not? Well, even on a human level, there are two kinds of pretending. There's a negative kind where pretense replaces reality, such as when someone pretends to help you instead of actually helping you. But there's also a positive kind where the pretense leads to the real thing. When you're not feeling particularly friendly but know you should be, the best thing you can do is often to put on a friendly manner and behave as if you were a kinder person than you actually are. And before you know it, you'll genuinely start feeling friendlier than before. Often, the only way to acquire a quality is to start behaving as if you already possess it. That's why children's games are so important. They always pretend to be grown-ups, playing soldiers, playing shop. But all the while, they are strengthening their muscles and sharpening their minds, so the pretense of being grown-up helps them truly grow up.

Now, the moment you realize "Here I am, pretending to be Christ," it's highly likely that you'll immediately see how you can make the pretense less artificial and more real at that very moment. You'll notice several things happening in your mind that wouldn't be there if you were truly a son of God. Well, stop them. Or you might realize that instead of saying your prayers, you should be downstairs writing a letter or helping your spouse with the dishes. Well, go and do it.

Do you see what's happening? Christ Himself, the Son of God who is both fully human (like you) and fully God (like His Father), is actually with you. At that very moment, He begins to transform your pretense into reality. This isn't just a fancy way of saying that your conscience is guiding you. If you only consult your conscience, you'll get one result but, if you remember that you're pretending to be Christ, you'll get a different one. There are many things that your conscience might not label as definitively wrong (especially things in your mind), but you'll realize that you can't continue doing them if you're genuinely trying to be like Christ. It's no longer just about right and wrong; you're striving to adopt the goodness of a Person. It's more like painting a portrait than obeying a set of rules. And here's the strange thing: while it may be harder than simply following rules in one way, it's actually easier in another.

The real Son of God is by your side. He's starting to turn you into someone like Himself. He's beginning to infuse His life, thoughts, His very essence, into you. He's transforming you from a mere tin soldier into a living person. The part of you that resists this change is the part that is still like tin.

Some of you may feel that this is unlike your own experience. You might say, "I've never felt helped by an invisible Christ, but I've often been helped by other human beings." That's similar to a woman in the war who claimed that a bread shortage wouldn't affect her household because they always ate toast. If there's no bread, there won't be any toast. If there were no help from Christ, there would be no help from other human beings. Christ works on us in various ways, not only through what we consider our "religious life." He works through nature, our own bodies, books, and sometimes even through experiences that seem contradictory to Christian beliefs. When a young person who has been attending church as a routine realizes honestly that they don't believe in Christianity and stops going (assuming it's for honesty's sake and not just to annoy their parents), the spirit of Christ is probably closer to them than ever before. But above all, He works on us through each other.

People are mirrors or carriers of Christ to one another, sometimes without even realizing it. This "good infection" can be transmitted by those who don't possess it themselves. People who weren't Christians themselves helped me discover Christianity. But usually, it's those who truly know Him that bring Him to others. That's why the Church, the entire community of Christians showing Christ to one another, is so important. You could say that when two Christians are following Christ together, it's not just twice as much Christianity as when they're apart, but sixteen times as much.

But don't forget this: at first, it's natural for a baby to drink its mother's milk without recognizing its mother. Similarly, it's natural for us to see the person who helps us without seeing Christ behind them. But we can't remain like babies. We must grow to recognize the true Giver. It would be foolish not to because if we don't, we'll be relying solely on human beings. And that will let us down. Even the best and wisest among them will make mistakes, and eventually, they'll all die. We should be grateful to the people who have helped us, honor and love them. But never, ever put our entire faith in any human being, even if they're the best and wisest person in the world. You can do many things with sand, but don't try to build a house on it.

Now we start to understand what the New Testament always talks about. It speaks of Christians being "born again," putting on Christ, having Christ formed in us, and gaining the mind of Christ.

Let go of the notion that these expressions merely mean that Christians should read what Christ said and try to follow it, like someone reading the works of Plato or Marx and attempting to put their ideas into practice. They mean something much deeper. They signify that a real Person, Christ, is here and now, in the same room where you're saying your prayers, actively working within you. It's not about a good man who died two thousand years ago. It's about a living Man who is just as human as you are and just as much God as He was when He created the world. He's genuinely present, intervening in your very being. He's destroying your old, natural self and replacing it with His own nature. Initially, this transformation may happen only for moments, but then it can extend to longer periods. Ultimately, if all goes well, it will permanently turn you into a different kind of being—a new little Christ. You'll have the same kind of life as God, sharing in His power, joy, knowledge, and eternity. And soon, you'll make two more discoveries.

First, you'll start to notice not just your specific sinful acts but your overall sinfulness. You'll become alarmed not only by what you do but also by what you are. Let me explain using my own experience. When I come to my evening prayers and try to evaluate my sins of the day, nine times out of ten, the most obvious one is some act against kindness. I've sulked, snapped, sneered, snubbed, or stormed. And my immediate excuse is usually that the provocation was sudden and unexpected—I was caught off guard and didn't have time to compose myself. Now, that may lessen the severity of those particular acts, as they would have been worse if I had intentionally planned them. However, doesn't what a person does when caught off guard reveal their true character? Isn't what surfaces before they have a chance to put on a facade the truth? If there are rats in a cellar, you're most likely to spot them if you suddenly enter. But the suddenness doesn't create the rats; it just prevents them from hiding. Similarly, the suddenness of the provocation doesn't make me an ill-tempered person; it simply shows me that I am. The rats of resentment and vindictiveness are always present in the cellar of my soul. Unfortunately, that cellar is beyond the reach of my conscious will. I can to some extent control my actions, but I have no direct control over my temperament. And as I mentioned earlier, what we are matters even more than what we do. Our actions primarily serve as evidence of our true character. Therefore, the change I most need to undergo is one that my voluntary efforts alone cannot achieve. This also applies to my good actions. How many of them were genuinely motivated? How many were driven by fear of public opinion or a desire to show off? How many resulted from stubbornness or a sense of superiority, which in different circumstances might have led to very negative acts? I can't simply will myself to have new motives. After the initial steps in the Christian journey, we realize that only God can truly accomplish what needs to be done within our souls.

And this brings us to something that has been misleading in my previous statements.

Secondly, I've been speaking as if it's us who do everything. In reality, it's God who does everything. At most, we allow Him to work in us. In a sense, you could even say that it's God who pretends. The Three-Personal God envisions a self-centered, greedy, grumbling, rebellious human being in front of Him. Yet, He says, "Let's pretend that this isn't just a mere creature but our Son. It's like Christ to the extent that it's a human, as He became human. Let's pretend that it's also like Him in spirit. Let's treat it as if it were what it actually isn't. Let's pretend in order to make the pretense a reality." God sees you as if you were a little Christ, and Christ stands beside you, transforming you into one. I understand that this concept of divine make-believe might sound strange at first. But is it truly so strange? Isn't this how the higher elevates the lower? A mother teaches her baby to talk by speaking to it as if it understands, long before it actually does. We treat our dogs as if they were "almost human," and eventually, they become "almost human."

IS CHRISTIANITY HARD OR EASY?

In the previous chapter, we discussed the concept of "putting on Christ," which means pretending to be a son of God in order to eventually become a true son. I want to clarify that this is not just one of the many tasks that Christians have to do, nor is it an exclusive exercise for a select few. It encompasses the entirety of Christianity. Christianity offers nothing else. I would like to explain how it differs from ordinary notions of "morality" and "being good."

Before becoming Christians, we all have a common understanding. We start with our ordinary selves, with our various desires and interests. Then, we acknowledge that something else, which we may call "morality," "decent behavior," or "the good of society," makes demands on our self that conflict with our desires. "Being good" means yielding to those demands. Some of the things our natural self wanted to do turn out to be "wrong," so we have to give them up. Other things that our self didn't want to do turn out to be "right," so we must do them. However, we hope that once all the demands have been met, our natural self will still have a chance and some time to pursue its own life and do what it wants. Essentially, we are like an honest person who pays their taxes but hopes to have enough left over to live on. We still view our natural self as the starting point.

As long as we think that way, one of two outcomes is likely to occur. Either we give up trying to be good, or we become extremely unhappy. Let's be clear: if you truly strive to meet all the demands placed on your natural self, you won't have enough left over to sustain it. The more you obey your conscience, the more it will demand from you. And your natural self, which is being starved, hindered, and constantly worried, will become increasingly angry. Eventually, you will either give up trying to be good or become one of those people who "live for others" but in a discontented and complaining manner, always wondering why others don't appreciate it more and constantly playing the martyr. Once you reach that point, you'll be a greater burden to those around you than if you had simply remained self-centered.

The Christian path is different—it is both harder and easier. Christ says, "Give me everything. I don't just want your time, money, and work. I want you. I haven't come to torment your natural self; I've come to destroy it. Half-hearted efforts won't do any good. I don't want to prune a few branches here and there; I want the whole tree to come down. I don't want to drill, crown, or fill the tooth; I want it extracted. Surrender your entire natural self—all your desires that you consider innocent as well as the ones you consider wicked. I will give you a new self in return. In fact, I will give you Myself—my own will shall become yours."

This path is both harder and easier than what we are all attempting to do. You may have noticed that Christ Himself sometimes describes the Christian path as very difficult and at other times as very easy. He says, "Take up your Cross"—in other words, it's like being beaten to death in a concentration camp. Yet, the next moment He says, "My yoke is easy, and my burden is light." He means both statements, and we can understand why.

Teachers will tell you that the laziest student in the class is the one who ends up working the hardest. They mean that if you give two students a geometry problem to solve, the one willing to put in the effort will try to understand it. The lazy student will try to memorize the solution because, at that moment, it requires less effort. But six months later, when they are preparing for an exam, the lazy student will be toiling away for hours on things the other student understood and enjoyed within minutes. Laziness ultimately results in more work. This can be viewed in another way. In battle or mountain climbing, there is often a daring action that requires a lot of courage, but in the long run, it is the safest course of action. If you shy away from it, you will find yourself in far greater danger hours later. The cowardly choice is also the most perilous.

The same principle applies here. The truly difficult and almost impossible thing is to surrender your entire self — your desires and precautions — to Christ. Yet, it is far easier than what we are all trying to do instead. What we are attempting is to remain what we consider our "true selves," to make personal happiness our primary goal in life, while still trying to be "good." We want our mind and heart to pursue their own desires — whether it's money, pleasure, or ambition — while hoping to act honestly, chastely, and humbly. However, this is precisely what Christ warned us we cannot do. As He said, a thistle cannot produce figs. If I am a field that only contains grass seeds, I cannot yield wheat. Trimming the grass may keep it short, but I will still produce grass and not wheat. If I want to produce wheat, the transformation must go deeper than the surface. I must be plowed and replanted.

That's why the real challenge of the Christian life arises in a place where people don't usually look for it: the moment we wake up each morning. Our desires and hopes for the day rush at us like wild animals. The first task each morning is simply to push them all back, to listen to that other voice, adopt that different perspective, and allow that larger, stronger, and calmer life to flow in. And we must continue doing this throughout the day—detaching ourselves from our natural fussing and worrying, seeking shelter from the wind.

At first, we can only achieve this for brief moments. However, from those moments, the new kind of life will start to permeate our being because we are letting Christ work in the right part of us. It's like the difference between applying paint superficially and using a dye or stain that penetrates deeply. Christ never spoke in vague, idealistic terms. When He said, "Be perfect," He meant it. He meant that we must fully commit to the process. It is difficult, but the compromise we often desire is even harder—in fact, it's impossible. It may be challenging for an egg to transform into a bird, but it would be even more difficult for it to learn to fly while remaining an egg. Currently, we are like eggs. We cannot indefinitely remain ordinary, decent eggs. We must hatch or we will spoil.

Allow me to reiterate what I mentioned earlier: this is the entirety of Christianity. There is nothing else. It's easy to become confused about that. It's easy to think that the Church has various objectives—education, construction, missions, conducting services—similar to how it's easy to think that the State has multiple objectives—military, political, economic, and so on. But in reality, things are much simpler. The State exists solely to promote and safeguard the ordinary happiness of human beings in this life. It could be a husband and wife chatting by the fire, friends playing darts in a pub, or an individual reading a book or gardening in their own space—that is the purpose of the State. If actions don't contribute to enhancing, prolonging, and protecting such moments, all the laws, parliaments, armies, courts, police, economics, and so on are merely a waste of time. Similarly, the Church exists for no other reason than to bring people into Christ, to transform them into little Christs. If it fails to do so, all the cathedrals, clergy, missions, sermons, and even the Bible itself are simply futile.

God became Man for no other purpose. It's even debatable whether the entire universe was created for any other purpose. The Bible states that the entire universe was made for Christ and that everything will be gathered together in Him. We don't know what lives in parts of the universe millions of miles away from Earth. Even on Earth, we don't understand how it applies to things other than humans. After all, the plan has only been revealed to us in relation to ourselves.

Sometimes, I like to imagine that this concept might apply to other things. I believe I can see how higher animals, in a way, become more human when humans love them and make them so. I can even see how lifeless objects and plants become part of humanity when humans study, use, and appreciate them. If intelligent beings exist on other worlds, they might do the same with their worlds. It's possible that when intelligent creatures unite with Christ, they would bring along all other things. However, it's merely speculation. What we have been told is how we, as humans, can be united with Christ—become part of that incredible gift that the young Prince of the universe wants to present to His Father, which is Himself and therefore us in Him. It is the only purpose for which we were created. The Bible provides intriguing hints that when we are drawn into Christ, many other things in nature will also be set right. The nightmare will end, and a new day will dawn.

COUNTING THE COST

I've noticed that many people have been troubled by what I said in the previous chapter regarding the words of Our Lord, "Be ye perfect." Some individuals seem to interpret this as meaning, "I won't help you unless you are perfect," and since we can't achieve perfection, they believe our situation is hopeless. However, I don't think that's what He meant. I believe He meant, "The only assistance I will provide is to help you become perfect. You may desire something less, but I won't offer anything less."

Let me explain with an analogy. When I was a child and had a toothache, I knew that if I went to my mother, she would give me something to alleviate the pain for that night so I could sleep. However, I hesitated to go to her, at least until the pain became unbearable. The reason was that I knew she wouldn't just provide the pain relief; she would also take me to the dentist the next morning. I couldn't obtain what I wanted from her without receiving something more that I didn't desire. I wanted immediate relief, but I couldn't have it without having my teeth properly fixed. And I knew those dentists; I knew they would start tinkering with other teeth that weren't yet causing me any pain. They wouldn't leave well enough alone; if you gave them an inch, they took a mile.

Now, in a similar way, Our Lord is like those dentists. If you give Him an inch, He will take a mile. Many people approach Him seeking healing from a specific sin they are ashamed of, such as masturbation or cowardice, or a sin that is clearly causing problems in their daily lives, such as anger or drunkenness. He will indeed heal that specific sin, but He won't stop there. That may be all you asked for, but if you invite Him in, He will provide you with the complete treatment.

That's why He cautioned people to "count the cost" before becoming Christians. "Make no mistake," He says, "if you allow me, I will make you perfect. The moment you surrender yourself to Me, that's what you're signing up for. Nothing less or different. You have free will, and if you choose, you can push Me away. But if you don't push Me away, understand that I am committed to seeing this process through. No matter the suffering it may entail in your earthly life or the inconceivable purification it may require after death, no matter the cost to Me, I will never cease or let you rest until you are truly perfect — until my Father can wholeheartedly declare His pleasure in you, just as He expressed His satisfaction with Me. This is what I can and will do. But I won't settle for anything less."

Yet, here's the other equally important aspect of it: this Helper who will ultimately be satisfied with nothing less than absolute perfection will also be delighted with your initial feeble and stumbling efforts to fulfill even the simplest duty tomorrow. As the great Christian writer George MacDonald pointed out, every father is pleased when his baby takes its first steps, but no father would be satisfied with anything less than a steady, confident, and mature walk from his adult son. Similarly, he said, "God is easy to please but hard to satisfy."

The practical implication is this: On one hand, we must never assume that our own unaided efforts will be sufficient to keep us on the path of righteousness even for the next twenty-four hours. Without His support, none of us is safe from committing serious sins. On the other hand, no degree of holiness or heroism ever displayed by the greatest saints is beyond what He is determined to cultivate in each one of us eventually. The process won't be completed in this life, but He intends to bring us as close as possible to that point before our death.

That's why we shouldn't be surprised if we encounter hardships. When a person turns to Christ and seems to be progressing well, with some of their bad habits corrected, they often expect that things should now go smoothly. However, they may be disappointed when difficulties arise — illnesses, financial problems, new temptations. They wonder why these things are happening. It's because God is propelling them to a higher level, putting them in situations where they must display even greater courage, patience, or love than they ever imagined. To us, it may seem unnecessary, but that's because we haven't grasped the tremendous transformation He intends for us.

Let me share another parable from George MacDonald. Imagine yourself as a house. God comes to renovate that house. Initially, you understand the repairs and improvements He's making — fixing the plumbing, patching the leaky roof, and so on. Those tasks were obvious and expected. But then He starts knocking down walls in a way that is painful and seems nonsensical. You may wonder, "What on earth is He doing?" The explanation is that He is constructing an entirely different house from what you had envisioned — adding new wings, extra floors, towers, and courtyards. You thought you were going to be transformed into a modest cottage, but He is building a majestic palace. He intends to dwell in it Himself.

The command "Be ye perfect" is not a lofty ideal or an impossible demand. He will make us into beings capable of obeying that command. In the Bible, He proclaimed that we are "gods," and He will fulfill His words. If we allow Him (because we can choose to resist), He will transform even the weakest and most sinful among us into godlike creatures — radiant, immortal beings pulsating with boundless energy, joy, wisdom, and love. We can't fully comprehend it now, but we will become bright mirrors reflecting His power, delight, and goodness on a smaller scale. The process will be long and, at times, painful, but that's what we're destined for. Nothing less. He meant what He said.

NICE PEOPLE OR NEW MEN

He meant what He said. Those who surrender themselves to Him will become perfect, just as He is perfect—perfect in love, wisdom, joy, beauty, and immortality. However, this transformation won't be completed during our lifetime, as death is an integral part of the process. We can't be certain how far the change will have progressed for each individual Christian before their death.

Now, let's address a common question that arises: If Christianity is true, why aren't all Christians noticeably nicer than non-Christians? This question contains both reasonable and unreasonable aspects. The reasonable part is this: If someone's conversion to Christianity doesn't lead to any improvement in their outward behavior—if they continue to be snobbish, spiteful, envious, or ambitious—then it's valid to suspect that their "conversion" was mostly imaginary. Every time a person thinks they have made progress after their initial conversion, that's the test to apply. Fine feelings, new insights, and increased interest in religion mean nothing if they don't result in better actual behavior. Just like in an illness, feeling better isn't significant if the thermometer shows that your temperature is still rising. In that sense, the outside world is justified in evaluating Christianity based on its results. Christ Himself instructed us to judge by results. A tree is known by its fruit, and 'the proof of the pudding is in the eating'. When we Christians behave poorly or fail to behave well, we make Christianity appear unbelievable to those outside. During the war, posters reminded us that careless talk costs lives. It is equally true that careless lives cost talk. Our careless lives provoke conversations in the outside world that cast doubt on the truth of Christianity itself.

However, there is another way in which the outside world may demand results that is quite illogical. They may demand not only that each person's life improves when they become Christians but also that the whole world be neatly divided into two groups — Christians and non-Christians — and that everyone in the Christian camp should be clearly nicer than everyone in the non-Christian camp at any given moment. This expectation is unreasonable for several reasons.

Firstly, the situation in the actual world is much more complex than that. The world isn't divided into 100% Christians and 100% non-Christians. There are many individuals who are gradually ceasing to identify as Christians but still label themselves as such, including some clergy members. There are others who are gradually becoming Christians without acknowledging it yet. There are people who don't fully embrace the Christian doctrine concerning Christ but are strongly drawn to Him in a deeper sense than they realize. There are people in other religions who are led by God's secret influence to focus on aspects of their faith that align with Christianity, making them belong to Christ unknowingly. For example, a Buddhist with goodwill may increasingly concentrate on the Buddhist teaching of mercy while leaving other aspects in the background, even though they might still claim to believe in them. Many morally upright individuals from pre-Christian times may have been in a similar position. Additionally, many people simply have confused beliefs and inconsistent convictions mixed together. Consequently, it is not very helpful to make general judgments about Christians and non-Christians. It is more useful to compare cats and dogs or even men and women because in those cases, we know definitively which is which. Animals don't transform from being dogs into cats, slowly or suddenly. However, when we compare Christians in general with non-Christians in general, we often aren't thinking about real people we actually know but rather about vague ideas we've derived from novels and newspapers. To compare a bad Christian with a good Atheist, you need to consider real individuals you've met. Otherwise, it's a waste of time.

Secondly, let's imagine we've narrowed down the comparison to two real people in our own community, not imaginary Christians and non-Christians. Even in that case, we need to ask the right question. If Christianity is true, then it should follow that (a) any Christian will be nicer than they would be if they weren't a Christian, and (b) anyone who becomes a Christian will be nicer than they were before. Similarly, if the advertisements for a toothpaste called White Smile are true, it should follow that (a) anyone who uses it will have better teeth than they would without using it, and (b) if someone starts using it, their teeth will improve. But pointing out that I, as a user of White Smile (and also someone with genetically poor teeth), don't have as perfect a set of teeth as a healthy young person who has never used toothpaste doesn't, by itself, prove that the advertisements are false. Christian Jane Bates may have a more unkind tongue than unbeliever Dick Firkin, but that alone doesn't determine whether Christianity works. The crucial question is what Jane's tongue would be like if she weren't a Christian and what Dick's would be like if he became one. Jane and Dick possess certain temperaments resulting from natural causes and early upbringing. Christianity claims to subject both temperaments to new management if they allow it to do so. What you have the right to ask is whether that management, if given control, improves the individuals. It's widely known that the management of Dick's temperament is much "nicer" than the management of Jane's. However, that's not the point. When evaluating the management of a factory, one must consider not only the output but also the machinery. Factory A may be a marvel for producing anything at all, given its plant. Factory B may have first-rate equipment, yet its output may be far lower than expected. Undoubtedly, the capable manager of Factory A will introduce new machinery as soon as possible, but that takes time. In the meantime, low output doesn't prove the manager's failure.

Thirdly, let's delve a little deeper. The manager plans to introduce new machinery. Before Christ is finished with Jane, she will become a truly "nice" person. However, if we stop there, it may give the impression that Christ's only objective is to elevate Jane to the same level that Dick has always been on. In fact, we've been speaking as if Dick is already fine and dandy, as if Christianity is something that nasty people need, while nice people can do without it, and as if niceness is all God demands. Yet, this would be a grave mistake. The truth is that in God's eyes, Dick Firkin needs "saving" just as much as Jane does.

In one sense (which I'll explain shortly), niceness hardly matters. We can't expect God to view Dick's calm temperament and friendly disposition exactly as we do. These qualities are the result of natural causes that God Himself creates. They are a gift from God to Dick, not something Dick bestows upon God. Similarly, God has allowed natural causes to work in a world tainted by centuries of sin, resulting in Jane's narrow-mindedness and frazzled nerves, which contribute to her unpleasant behavior. In His own time, God intends to correct those aspects of her nature. However, that isn't what concerns God most. It presents no difficulties for Him. It's not what He is anxious about. What He watches, waits for, and works towards is something even challenging for God because, by the nature of the matter, He cannot achieve it through a mere act of power. He watches, waits for, and works towards this outcome in both Jane Bates and Dick Firkin. It is something they can freely give or freely withhold from Him. Will they choose to turn to Him and fulfill the sole purpose for which they were created? Their free will trembles inside them like the needle of a compass. However, it's a needle that can choose its direction. It can point towards true North, but it doesn't have to. Will it point North? That is the crucial question. God can assist the needle in doing so, but He cannot force it. He cannot, so to speak, reach out and directly manipulate it into the right position, as that would negate free will. Will it point to God? This is what everything hinges upon.

God can help the needle to align with Him. However, He cannot force it. He cannot impose His will upon us without compromising our free will. Whether the needle points towards God depends on the individual's choice. He can influence it, but it remains a voluntary decision.

THE NEW MEN

In the last chapter, I compared Christ's work of transforming people into "New Men" to the process of turning a horse into a winged creature. I used that extreme example to emphasize that it is not just about improvement but a complete transformation. A similar parallel can be found in the natural world through the remarkable transformations we can induce in insects using specific rays. Some people speculate that this is how evolution works, with external rays causing changes in creatures. Once these alterations occur, natural selection comes into play, with the useful changes surviving and the others getting eliminated.

To better understand the Christian idea, we can relate it to the concept of evolution. Nowadays, almost everyone is aware of evolutionary theory, although there are still some educated individuals who doubt it. It is widely supposed that humans have evolved from lower forms of life. As a result, people often wonder what the next step in evolution will be and when something beyond man will appear. Some imaginative writers try to envision this next step, often referred to as the "Superman." However, their depictions usually end up portraying someone even nastier than humans, with extra limbs or exaggerated features. But what if the next step is something even more different from what they have imagined? Isn't it likely to be so?

Thousands of centuries ago, enormous, heavily armored creatures evolved. Observing the course of evolution at that time, one would have expected it to continue toward even heavier armor. However, that prediction would have been wrong. The future held a surprise that no one could have foreseen. It introduced small, naked, unarmored animals with superior brains, and with those brains, they would come to dominate the entire planet. They were not just going to possess more power than the prehistoric monsters; they would have a completely new kind of power. The next step would not only be different but different in an entirely new way. The stream of evolution was not going to follow the direction that was apparent at the time; it was going to take a sharp turn.

It seems to me that most popular speculations about the next step in evolution are making a similar mistake. People observe or believe they see men developing greater intelligence and increasing their mastery over nature. Because they perceive the current trend in that direction, they assume it will continue in the same path. However, I can't help but think that the next step will be genuinely new, moving in a direction that no one could have imagined. Otherwise, it wouldn't be worth calling it a "New Step." I would expect not just a difference but a new kind of difference. I would anticipate not merely a change but a new method of bringing about that change. To put it paradoxically, I would expect the next stage in evolution not to be an evolution at all; I would expect evolution itself, as a method of producing change, to be surpassed. And finally, I wouldn't be surprised if very few people noticed when this transformation actually occurred.

If we discuss it in these terms, the Christian view precisely asserts that the next step has already happened, and it is genuinely new. It is not merely a change from intelligent men to even more intelligent men; it is a change that goes in a completely different direction—a shift from being creatures of God to becoming His sons. The first instance of this change occurred in Palestine two thousand years ago. In a sense, this change is not "evolution" at all because it is not an outcome of the natural process of events, but rather something coming into nature from outside. However, that is exactly what I would expect. Our understanding of evolution is based on studying the past, so if there are real novelties in store, our past-based idea will not fully account for them. Moreover, this new step differs from all previous ones not only in its origin outside of nature but also in several other aspects.

(1) This step does not involve sexual reproduction. Should we be surprised by that? There was a time before sex existed, and development would have had to occur through different methods. Therefore, it could have been expected that sex would eventually disappear or, as is actually happening, cease to be the primary means of development while still remaining in existence.

(2) In earlier stages, living organisms had little or no choice when it came to taking the new step. Progress primarily happened to them rather than being something they actively pursued. However, the new step, the transition from being creatures to being sons, is voluntary, at least in a sense. It is not voluntary in the sense that we could have chosen it on our own or even imagined it, but it is voluntary in the sense that when it is presented to us, we can choose to accept or reject it. We have the option to shrink back, dig in our heels, and allow the new humanity to proceed without our participation.

(3) I referred to Christ as the "first instance" of the new man. However, He is much more than that. He is not merely a new man, a single specimen of the species, but the embodiment of the new man. He is the origin, center, and life of all the new men. He entered the created universe willingly, bringing with Him the Zoe, the new life (new to us, of course, as Zoe has existed eternally in its own place). He transmits this new life not

through heredity but through what I described as "good infection." Everyone who receives it does so through personal contact with Him. Others become "new" by being "in Him."

(4) This step occurs at a different pace compared to previous ones. When considering the development of mankind on this planet, the spread of Christianity throughout the human race seems to happen rapidly, like a flash of lightning. Two thousand years is almost insignificant in the grand history of the universe. We must not forget that we are still in the early stages of Christianity. The divisions and conflicts among us, which are currently wicked and wasteful, are hopefully just temporary issues that will resolve as we mature. The outer world may perceive the opposite, thinking that Christianity is nearing its end. However, it has been proven wrong every time. The world has thought Christianity was dying due to external persecution or internal corruption, with the rise of other religions like Islam or scientific advancements or anti-Christian revolutionary movements. Yet, each time, Christianity has survived. Its first disappointment was over the crucifixion, but the Man came back to life. In a sense, this has been happening ever since. They keep trying to eliminate what He started, but every time they think it's dead and buried, they hear that it's still alive and has emerged in a new place. No wonder they hate us.

(5) The stakes are higher now. Falling back at earlier stages meant losing, at worst, a few years of life on Earth, and often not even that. However, by falling back at this particular step, we lose a prize that is infinitely valuable. The critical moment has arrived. Century by century, God has guided nature to the point where creatures can be taken out of nature and transformed into "gods" if they choose to be. It is akin to the crisis of birth. Until we rise and follow Christ, we remain part of nature, still in the womb of our great mother. Her pregnancy has been long, painful, and filled with anxiety, but it has reached its climax.

The crucial moment has come, and everything is ready. The Doctor has arrived. Will the birth go smoothly? However, it differs from a regular birth in one important aspect. In a typical birth, the baby has little choice; here, it has a choice. I wonder what an ordinary baby would do if it had the option. It might prefer to stay in the dark, warmth, and safety of the womb, thinking it is secure there. However, that would be a mistaken belief because if it remains there, it will die.

In this perspective, the new step has already taken place and is ongoing. New men, who have undergone this transformation, can be found scattered across the earth. Some may not be easily recognizable, but others can be identified. Every now and then, you come across them. You can tell they are different from us by their voices and faces; they appear stronger, calmer, happier, and more radiant. They operate on a different level than most of us. They are recognizable, but you need to know what to look for. They don't seek attention for themselves. You might think you're being kind to them, but in reality, they are the ones showing kindness to you. They love you more than other people do, but they are less dependent on you. (We need to let go of the desire to be needed, as it can be a challenging temptation to resist, especially for good-hearted individuals, especially women.) They often seem to have an abundance of time, and you may wonder where it comes from. Once you recognize one of them, it becomes easier to recognize the others. And I strongly suspect (though I cannot be certain) that they recognize one another immediately and unfailingly, transcending barriers of color, gender, class, age, and even religious beliefs. In a way, becoming holy is like joining a secret society. At the very least, it must be a great source of joy.

However, it's important not to think that all the new men are exactly alike in the usual sense. Some of what I've discussed in this book might lead you to believe that they would be.

Becoming new men means letting go of what we currently consider as our "selves." We must transition from being focused on ourselves to being united with Christ. His will should become our own, and we should think His thoughts, as the Bible says, to "have the mind of Christ." If Christ is one and is meant to be "in" all of us, wouldn't we then all be the same? It might sound that way, but in reality, it's not the case.

Finding a good illustration is difficult here because there is no other relationship quite like that between the Creator and one of His creatures. Nonetheless, I'll attempt two imperfect illustrations that may provide a glimpse of the truth. Imagine a group of people who have always lived in darkness. You try to describe to them what light is like. You might explain that if they step into the light, the same light would fall on all of them, and they would become visible, reflecting that light. They might imagine that since they all receive the same light and react to it in the same way (by reflecting it), they would all look alike. However, you and I know that the light would actually reveal how different they are. Another example is someone who knows nothing about salt. You give them a pinch to taste, and they experience a distinct strong, sharp flavor. Then you tell them that people in your country use salt in all their cooking. They might respond, "In that case, I suppose all your dishes taste exactly the same because the taste of that strong stuff you just gave me will overpower the taste of everything else." But you and I know that the real effect of salt is quite the opposite. Instead of masking the taste of eggs, tripe, or cabbage, it enhances their flavors. Their true tastes are brought out by the addition of salt. (Of course, I must warn you that this is not a perfect illustration because you can indeed ruin the taste of other things by using too much salt, whereas you cannot diminish the uniqueness of a human personality by having too much Christ. I'm doing my best here.)

It's similar with Christ and us. The more we remove what we currently consider as ourselves and allow Him to take over, the more authentically ourselves we become. Christ's abundance is such that millions and millions of "little Christs," each unique, would still be inadequate to fully express Him. He created all of them. He, like an author creating characters in a novel, invented all the different individuals that you and I were meant to be. In that sense, our true selves are waiting for us in Him. Trying to "be myself" without Him is futile. The more I resist Him and try to live solely for myself, the more I become influenced by my genetics, upbringing, surroundings, and natural desires. In reality, what I proudly call "Myself" becomes a convergence point for events I never initiated and cannot control. What I refer to as "My wishes" are merely desires arising from my physical body or influenced by the thoughts of others, or even suggested to me by devils. Eggs, alcohol, or a good night's sleep can be the real origins of what I arrogantly perceive as my own highly personal and discerning decision to engage romantically with the person sitting across from me on a train. Propaganda can be the true origin of what I consider my own personal political ideals. In my natural state, I am far from being the individual I like to believe I am. Most of what I consider "me" can be easily explained. It's when I turn to Christ, surrendering to His Personality, that I begin to develop a genuine sense of self. Earlier, I mentioned the existence of Personalities within God. Now I'll go a step further and state that there are no real personalities anywhere else. Until you let go of your self and surrender to Him, you won't possess a true self. Sameness is more prevalent among those who are most "natural," not among those who yield to Christ. How strikingly similar all the great tyrants and conquerors have been, while the saints are gloriously different.

However, there must be a genuine relinquishment of the self. You must cast it aside, almost blindly. Christ will indeed grant you a genuine personality, but you shouldn't seek Him for that reason alone. If you're preoccupied with your own personality, you aren't truly seeking Him at all. The very first step is to try to forget about the self entirely. Your real and new self, which is both Christ's and yours (and only yours because it is His), will not emerge as long as you are actively searching for it. It will appear when you are searching for Him instead. Does that sound strange? The same principle applies to everyday matters. Even in social interactions, you won't make a good impression on others if you constantly worry about the impression you're making. In literature and art, a person who fixates on being original will never achieve true originality. However, if you simply strive to tell the truth (without caring whether it has been said before countless times), you will often become original without even realizing it. This principle applies to all aspects of life. Surrender your self, and you will discover your authentic self. Lose your life, and you will save it. Embrace the daily deaths of your ambitions and cherished desires, and eventually, the death of your entire body, with every fiber of your being. In doing so, you will find eternal life. Withhold nothing. Nothing that you haven't given away will ever truly be yours. Nothing within you that hasn't died will ever experience resurrection.

THE END

ENDNOTES AND PERSONAL AFTERTHOUGHTS

ⁱ Page 32. Lewis wrote "One of the notable features of humanity's real moral judgment (as distinct from their mere chatter) is that they regard certain actions as being intrinsically right or wrong."

In my book, *WHAT DOES LOVE REQUIRE OF ME?* I presented a similar argument:

Our moral thinking comes more from intuition than from reason. Things just seem right or wrong to us.

Imagine a situation where the family dog dies, the family decides to bury the dog in the backyard and plant a memorial tree close by. Most of us instinctively think that this sounds reasonable and unobjectionable, even good. Now consider a slightly different scenario. The family decides to bury the dog in the back yard but first, they will make a meal of the dog and then bury the remains. Is that right? Most of us would consider the latter scenario as being repulsive.

We don't have a reason, a moral rule, for distinguishing between these two scenarios, it is by intuition we come to this thinking. In recent years these primary intuitions have changed. It is as if we have moral taste buds and those taste buds have shifted. The following are the primary factors that shape most people's moral intuitions.

- Is it harmful or not?
- Is it going to harm other people?[35]

---

[35] E.g., the fallout from the AIDS epidemic, refusing to where a mask during COVID, etc.?

- If something is not harmful it is hard for us to think that it is wrong.
- Is it freeing or oppressive?

Is it fair or is it discriminatory?

◆ ◆ ◆

ii Page 40. Repentance:

The best analogy I can give is... true repentance is like going to the dentist and having that bothersome molar removed and then realizing that you had completely forgotten what it was like to be free from pain for a very long time. I endured a spiritual toothache that lasted for the first 35 years of my life.

For most of us, the need to learn to ask for repentance should probably start around the age of two, especially around the terrible twos! Our parents may endeavour to instil some discipline in us, but repentance is another whole matter entirely.

Discipline is typically for our benefit. The deterrence factor, often in the form of pain, enables us to quickly learn from it. Repentance on the other hand calls for an act of the will. My will. I need to change. *I want to change* because *I want to be in the centre of God's will*. Failing to be in the centre of God's will inevitably result in spiritual toothache.

Repentance, *Metanoia* in Greek, means *a change of mind*. In modern dictionaries, it is typically described as 'the activity [that it is a verb] of reviewing one's actions and feeling contrition or regret for past wrongs, which is accompanied by a commitment to change for the better.' Biblical repentance is the same — but different.

In Acts 2:11-18 we read,

> *"When they heard this, they had no further objections and praised God, saying, "So then, even*

> *to Gentiles God has <u>granted</u> repentance that leads to life."*

The word for *granted*, as used here, is the Greek word *didomi*, which literally means to give [or to grant] to the one asking.

The God who created us knows full well that most of us are incapable of true repentance, and that He needed to make it a gift for us to be able to receive it and act upon it. He needs to be the initiator, the one who can *fully enable us* to repent, to turn around, to leave the past behind, to start in a new direction — the direction in which Christ is moving and for us to follow Him wherever He may lead.

This change in direction may come with *remorse* and *sorrow*, but don't dwell on these for too long. Whatever might have been their cause, it was dealt with on the Cross of Calvary! God's primary interest now is to help you change direction, for you to follow Him where He wants to take you, *"To have life and have it to the full"* is how Someone very special put it.

iii Page 139 "You must do this because I can't."

Back in 1986 I had been president of a successful audiovisual company in Toronto, Canada. I had two partners and we had approximately twenty-five employees. We had been 'living the highlife' until it suddenly came crashing down. To cut a long story short, our pride and arrogance eventually caught up with us. One evening, in the midst of this crash, I yelled out at the top of my lungs, "God, if you're there, help me!"

Even as the word "...me!" was coming out of my mouth, the phone rang. No, it wasn't God, just one of His servants who called to offer me words of encouragement. I knew it was too little, too late, but the uncanny timing caught my attention.

Don't ask me how, but in that moment, I knew God had heard me — and had responded.

That evening, for the first time in my life I prayed to God. Don't ask me what I prayed, I have absolutely no recollection, but in the days and weeks that followed I knew God existed and that, somehow or other, I knew that Jesus was 'It' and that God had indeed raised Him from the dead.

A short while later I went to a local restaurant with my next-door neighbours, Wayne and Barbara. We had become good friends. I forget the context of our conversation, but I do remember saying the words, "Since I have become a Christian..." In that moment the Holy Spirit showed up. The only way I can describe it is an overwhelming sense of peace and warmth. It was as though I had just gulped down a swig of the finest single-malt whiskey you can imagine and felt the warmth that radiates from within.

I must confess that in those few moments I had no idea what was happening to me. There was no doubt in my mind though that this was a 'God-thing'.

When I shared this experience with some friends, whom I knew to be Christians, they explained quoting Romans 10:9 from the Bible,

"If you confess with your mouth that Jesus is Lord, and believe in your heart that God raised Him from the dead, you shall be saved."

I guess, in the middle of a Greek restaurant, in the village of Oak Ridges, I was saved!

I want to briefly interject to say that this was my experience. Not everyone will have had the same experience as me. There are probably many who read this testimony that have simply grown up knowing God and cannot remember a time when God was not present in their lives.

iv What happens when you receive Jesus as Lord and Savior?

The first thing you realize is that there is a God who cares about you. Personally. Intimately. Passionately.

You will experience a deep inner peace; unlike anything you have experienced before in your life.

You will become aware of the presence of God. That 'void' in your inner self will be filled. You will feel complete.

If you have been aware of sin in your life, having a feeling of being unforgivable and worthless, you will feel a tremendous weight lifted from your shoulders. You will know God has forgiven you.

You will feel a sense of excitement and a desire to share your experience with others.

You may experience what feels like a physical hunger to read the Bible and, as you read it, you will find the words on the page come alive, as though God were speaking to you directly [which He is in fact doing].

You will experience a strong desire to praise and worship God.

You will notice that as you pray you begin to see your prayers being answered, often in ways that will confound and amaze you.

Over time, as you study, you will better understand the concepts and promises of the Bible, that when you accept Jesus as your Savior, He indwells you in the person of the Holy Spirit.

In time you will recognize and understand the 'spiritual gifts' God gives you.

As the Scripture says,

"Anyone who trusts in him will never be put to shame."

Romans 10:11

◆ ◆ ◆

ᵛ Page 139. Zero hour.

Maybe the words of C.S. Lewis have struck a chord of reason for you in this book, and logic and reason have brought you to this point. Maybe you have felt God tugging at your heartstrings and you feel the need to respond. Perhaps you are now like I was, hitting absolute bottom, feeling nothing but despair and desperation, having nowhere else to turn. Now is your time to simply say, "Yes." To God.

> *Yet to all who did receive him, to those who believed in his name, he gave the right to become children of God—children born not of natural descent, nor of human decision or a husband's will, but born of God.*
>
> *John 1:12-13*

Before you pray, I would like to offer a couple of words of encouragement. First, it is not your words that God is most interested in—it is your heart. We use words to communicate our feelings and intent, but they are not what is of paramount importance.

Second, God makes things super simple for us—so simple that many find it hard to comprehend. Through the apostle, Paul, God says,

"If you confess with your mouth that Jesus is Lord and believe in your heart that God raised Him from the dead, you will be saved."

What is more, God *gives* us the faith to believe. Even in our struggles to grasp these concepts, God is right there alongside us. Not sure what to pray? You can make the following words your own right now.

> "Lord Jesus, for too long I've kept you out of my life. I know that I am a sinner and that I cannot save myself. No longer will I close the door when I hear you knocking. By faith, I gratefully receive your gift of salvation. I am ready to trust you as my Lord and Saviour. Thank you, Lord Jesus, for coming to earth. I believe you are the Son of God who died on the cross for my sins and rose from the dead. Thank you for bearing my sins and giving me the gift of eternal life. I believe your words are true. Come into my heart, Lord Jesus, and be my Savior. Amen[36]."

If you have prayed this prayer from the heart, congratulations! You are now a child of God!

◆ ◆ ◆

So that this special day will be remembered, you can record your commitment here:

Today, I invited Jesus to be my Lord and Saviour.

This _____ day of _____, 20____

Signed _____

You can contact the author here: dohauthor@gmail.com

_____

[36] The word 'amen' is of Hebrew origin. In modern English it means 'so be it'. In Revelation 3:14, Jesus is referred to as, "the Amen, the faithful and true witness, the beginning of God's creation."

The books shown on the following pages include original works by David Harrison, and 'translations' of classic works into everyday English specifically adapted for North American and international readers.

For volume copies of any of these books (10+) or to contact the author, please send an email to dohauthor@gmail.com

Paperback and Kindle titles available on Amazon.

amzn.to/46Fk5m

The Next 60 Seconds
ISBN 979-8329684261

Surprised by Joy
ISBN 979-8334874077

The Pilgrim's Progress
ISBN 979-8873999002

If God, Then...
ISBN 979-8872942214

Is Jesus God?
ISBN 979-8401914781

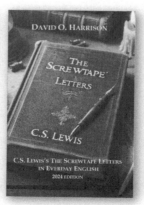

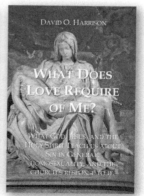

Mere Christianity
ISBN 979-8396258051

The Screwtape Letters
ISBN 979-8871578834

What Does Love Require?
ISBN 979-8767554140

Mere Christianity Student
ISBN 979-8327961340

THRIVE!
ISBN 979-8882973864

Large Print Editions

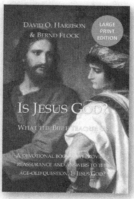

Pilgrim's Progress LPE
ISBN 979-8874359645

Is Jesus God? LPE
ISBN 9798877673564

Mere Christianity LPE
ISBN 979-8874349233

Paperback Group Study
Guides available on
Amazon.

amzn.to/46Fk5ml

Mere Christianity Student Study
ISBN 979-8328948142

THRIVE! Study Guide
ISBN 979-8321137420

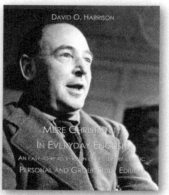

Mere Christianity Study Guide
ISBN 979-8326840851

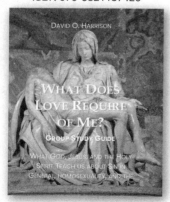

What Does Love Require Study
ISBN 979-8334819597

The Next 60 Seconds Study
ISBN 979-8329839869

Experience Narnia anew through the eyes of an author dedicated to making classic literature accessible and engaging for all.

Discover the enchanting world of Narnia in C.S. Lewis's beloved seven-book series, now beautifully adapted for today's young readers. This version brings the magic of Narnia to life in everyday English, making it more accessible while staying true to the original text. The author has carefully updated British idioms and vocabulary for North American and international audiences.

amazon.ca/dp/B0D9R24TML

Magician's Nephew
ISBN 979-8334248304

The Lion, the Witch...
ISBN 979-8333533319

The Horse and His Boy
ISBN 979-8333965660

Prince Caspian
ISBN 979-8334910706

The Dawn Trader
ISBN 979-8334177765

The Silver Chair
ISBN 979-8334495883

The Last Battle
ISBN 979-8334982413

Made in the USA
Middletown, DE
01 September 2024

60194651R00116